FEATHERS AT MY FEET

INDIGO RIVER
PUBLISHING

Feathers at my Feet

A MEMOIR OF
ENDURING FRIENDSHIP

BARBARA PEARSON

Editors: Pat Smith, Deborah Froese
Cover and Interior Design: Emma Elzinga

Indigo River Publishing
3 West Garden Street, Ste. 718
Pensacola, FL 32502
www.indigoriverpublishing.com

Ordering Information:
Quantity sales: Special discounts are available on quantity purchases by corporations, associations, and others. For details, contact the publisher at the address above.

Orders by US trade bookstores and wholesalers: Please contact the publisher at the address above.

Library of Congress Control Number: 2022909141
ISBN: 978-1-954676-30-5 (paperback) 978-1-954676-31-2 (ebook)

First Edition

With Indigo River Publishing, you can always expect great books, strong voices, and meaningful messages. Most importantly, you'll always find . . . words worth reading.

To Eleanor A. Pearson (1924 – 2019), in honor of the stories you told me about your beloved girlfriends at Sunnyside Park.

To Twyla, Pera, and Chloe, as you embark on your own journeys, may you experience the joys of special friendships.

And of course to Phyllis Bosco who encouraged us all to follow our bliss, thank you for the inspiration.

TABLE OF CONTENTS

CHAPTER 1

Serendipity

I KNEW OF Phyllis Bosco long before we actually met in 1980. An artist, teacher, and activist, she was a longstanding celebrity in my current hometown of Tallahassee, Florida. Her presence could be found everywhere from museums and galleries to the posters inside city buses. At every art show, her mixed-media pieces boogie-woogied while paintings displayed next to hers simply waltzed. A true Florida artist by upbringing and context, her art danced to magical mixtures of surf, sky, and sandbars. Splashes of turquoise. Splotches of flamingo pink. Sashes of aqua sewn directly into the canvas.

Phyllis's legendary past provided fodder for side comments from strangers who knew only her work and delicious long-winded accounts from people who knew her well. She had traveled to Mexico on Spring Break with three friends crammed into a VW bug. She'd protested against the Vietnam war with the Students for a Democratic Society (SDS) on the Florida State University campus and revolted against the "no pants" rule for women at the university's library. She'd left a salaried position to travel through Europe without income or a promise of a job when she returned. These are some of the stories etched in my mind; of course, there are many more.

At the time we met, I was a novice art teacher pushing an "art cart" (a classroom of supplies on wheels) along the covered walkways of one-story elementary schools. The classrooms lined up in rows like shoe boxes. To broaden my students' worldview, I showed them slides of African masks, Impressionist paintings, and Picasso's collages. I brought in fliers from art shows I had attended featuring work by local artists such as Phyllis Bosco. Back then, I couldn't imagine owning original art, much less one of her pieces.

One day a friend called. "I have a Phyllis Bosco," she said.

Jealousy hovered over my congratulatory words and questions. "Where did you get it? How much?" Shortly thereafter, I set aside money meant for groceries and purchased my own Phyllis Bosco at the LeMoyne Art Foundation. A wood-framed, five-by-seven abstract pastel that reminded me of a beach illuminated by a large sun or moon. I have it to this day.

At last, when serendipity brought Phyllis and me together, it was not in Tallahassee, a small college town where bumping into each other would have been natural, but on one of my trips to New York City to visit my mother. That summer, Democrats were affirming Jimmy Carter as their presidential nominee at Madison Square Garden. Phyllis's then husband, a journalist for the Associated Press, was covering the proceedings, and Phyllis could never resist a tagalong trip to the Big Apple.

She and I were both at the Whitney Museum flipping through postcards and prints in the gift shop. Adjacent to where we were standing was "Calder's Circus," a world of wire limbed clowns and yarn-maned lions. Engrossed in our own discoveries, oblivious to those around us, she and I collided.

"Hi," Phyllis said with a smile that stretched across her angular face. Her eyes sparkled. "Aren't you from Tallahassee?"

I gasped, grinning with delight that I had bumped into my favorite artist and astonished that she recognized me.

She leaned in from her shoulders, edging her face toward mine. Olive-toned skin, a strong nose, long limbed, the movement of an exotic bird. A small braid sectioned of long dark hair fell across her face.

"As a redhead you stand out in a crowd," she said, laughing into her words.

That's when I noticed her voice: high pitched but soft, full of breath, giggly but not silly, a whisper and a hum as if she were imparting—just to you—the most provocative secret.

"You look so familiar," she continued. "Have we met, maybe at an art show?"

"I am from Tallahassee, an art teacher, but I don't believe we've met. You're Phyllis, aren't you, the artist? I have one of your pieces, a small one. I love your work, and I . . ."

Phyllis smiled, but then moved on to other topics. She commented on the Democratic Convention and her husband's assignment, our country's general state of affairs, and the exhibits at the museum.

I nodded, adding a word here and there, but only half listening because I was so fascinated with her appearance. A flower child, for sure, with dangling peace-symbol earrings and fringed camel-colored boots. Layered vests: a tight one like a man's, and a tasseled loose one on top. When the strap of her hobo tote slipped from her shoulder, she scooted it back up with a twirl. Her hair, beads, and all that fringe rustled as if a summer breeze had miraculously whistled through the museum's lobby.

"Let's get together," she concluded, "when we get back."

"Yes, sure. Sure, yes, I'd like that." I beamed, feeling a bit giddy and sensing that somehow, I had crossed a threshold from my ordinary life into something spectacular.

CHAPTER 2

The Art Teacher

THE PATH THAT led me to Tallahassee and Phyllis's friendship involved rebellion, rootlessness, and discontent.

It started in New York during my last year of high school when Grandma proclaimed teaching as the perfect profession for me, and really, for all women. I held firm against that traditional female role. I was *not* going to be a teacher, or secretary, or nurse, period.

So, in the mid-1960s when I went to college to study art, I wandered from one program to another, left school only to return and quit again, wandered some more from one apartment and roommate to another, vacationed in Florida, met a man in a bar, and married him five months later.

Then the two of us wandered from one Boston apartment to another. A year later, our son was born; still we wandered. We packed our belongings into an old station wagon, drove south, and ended up on property east of Bithlo, Florida, where my husband tended beehives for the local Mormon Ranch. The job came with a house, rent free.

Soon we moved on, this time eighty miles southwest to Lakeland, an up-and-coming city with a minor league baseball team and a job opening with the Game and Fish Commission. Our second child was born at Lakeland General.

We lived in a cinderblock house with a carport on a corner lot with more dirt than grass. A white hunting dog—one I don't believe I ever petted—hunkered in a kennel at the back of the property. During the day, with the baby on my hip, I cut peanut butter sandwiches into triangles for our lunch. I could hear my older son giggling through the open window as he sailed plastic boats in our inflatable kiddie pool. Before sunset, my husband would roar his company-issued pickup truck onto the yard so the driveway was left open for play. At night while everyone slept, I wrote in my journal.

This lifestyle was fine for my Florida-raised husband, but much too "country" for this New Yorker. I valued art museums over fish hatcheries and preferred shops along boulevards to john boats on lakes. I longed for a community of like-minded, artistic, and forward-thinking friends. I also thought my husband should have a college degree.

I flipped through catalogues and poured over maps, and after much consideration, selected Florida State University in Tallahassee as the ideal place for him. He was accepted, and we moved into family student housing, but to my chagrin, my spouse rarely attended class. Instead, he jammed with local musicians.

For the first time, I realized what should have been obvious. I was the one who loved school, the energy of a college campus, and the preparation involved with establishing a career. So, I enrolled in the College of Education. Ten years after Grandma's proclamation about teaching, I discovered her wisdom.

Tallahassee became my nest, a secure home for me to grow and develop my talents. The metaphor was reinforced many years later when I saw the city from an airplane. The view at ten thousand feet showed Tallahassee encircled by a protective forest, fingers of green spreading out in all directions, and touched on one side by the silvery shimmer of the Gulf of Mexico. Insulated by its geography, but expansive in its outlook, Tallahassee, the state capital, proved to be a bright blue political dot. It was home to two universities; the site for the Miccosukee Land Co-op, an intentional community; and an overnight stop for music greats traveling between larger cities.

After receiving a Bachelor of Arts degree from FSU, I interviewed for a job at a local elementary school in a large, multi-purpose classroom. Principals without assigned art teachers sat in a semicircle while newly degreed applicants sat along one side of the room. A lone chair for the spotlighted job seeker faced the potential employers.

Nerves knotted my gut. A decade prior, I would have responded to the questions with jumbled words punctuated with *um's* and pauses, but motherhood had matured me, and I had a mission. Our family required at least one steady income just to get by.

A week later, I drove my light blue, rust-spotted Chevy to my teaching assignment, its trunk crammed with paint, markers, and blunt-edged scissors. Part time with two schools. Four classes for each K–5 grade level at both schools meant about seven hundred children total in four days at forty minutes per classroom. On Fridays, I created games and lessons while my children played outside with friends in the greenspace next to our apartment.

Feeling satisfied and fulfilled, I knew I had found my niche, but had yet to discover the comradery of a unique band of women friends. It would take four more years of focus on family and my newfound profession before I met Phyllis.

CHAPTER 3

The Dancing Girls

NOT LONG AFTER our fateful meeting in New York, Phyllis's marriage ended, but her chosen extended family remained intact: artists, art teachers, musicians—and people who knew artists and musicians—as well as pets, children, students, and older folk from the Senior Center. With her invitation to get together, I too became part of her world. It was that easy.

Over time, a core group of six women, ranging in age from late twenties to late thirties, emerged from this colorful patchwork community. Joan and Annie worked for the state government, and Carole and Kiki taught at FSU's research school. I taught in the public school system, and Phyllis—our nucleus—created art in all media, shapes, and forms.

We costumed for art shows, smoked cigarillos at weddings, and always danced. Our moniker, "The Dancing Girls," was bestowed upon us by a man we called "the Deacon."

At first, I only knew him as Phyllis's longtime friend. I'd find her in the kitchen trailing the longest phone cord ever as she tidied the room while talking to him. "It's the Deacon," she'd say, her hand momentarily covering the mouthpiece.

When they hung up, her eyes would twinkle, evidence I thought, of their mutual admiration for Democratic politics and each other's proclivities. Later, I learned about his distinguished life: reporter, the first on the scene at the 1963 Birmingham church bombing; speechwriter for the Carter Administration; Habitat for Humanity administrator; and then a hospital chaplain ministering to those with HIV/AIDS.

Perhaps Phyllis wanted to keep their status in the friendship zone when she arranged for six women, rather than just the two of them, to celebrate the Deacon's sixtieth birthday. When he walked into the kitchen through Phyllis's carport door—a slightly-built man with a gentle countenance, dressed in khakis and a plaid shirt—he encountered six women wearing tux jackets, no blouses, and bow ties. Stilettos click-click-clicked across the linoleum floor.

The Deacon gaped, then laughed, then turned to Phyllis as if to say, *What in the . . .?*

Phyllis interrupted. "We are your escorts for your birthday celebration. Happy Birthday." She doubled over with soundless laughter, a long hum dissolving into a soft *sssss*.

We made the rounds of Tallahassee college bars. When the Deacon drank a beer, six women lifted their mugs. Six women scrambled to light his cigar while puffing their own. When the Deacon decided to dance, six women flanked him through the crowd as other patrons cleared the dance floor and waved.

After the celebration, when the phone calls resumed, the Deacon, apparently tired of asking "How's Kiki, and how's Barbara, and how's . . .?" simply asked, "How are the Dancing Girls?" And it stuck. From then on, we called ourselves "the Dancing Girls."

When summer heat choked Tallahassee, we'd spend weekend days at Kiki's pool, an oasis of banana palms, myrtles, oaks, and outdoor sculptures. We'd languish on popsicle-colored rafts and breathe in tranquility—a strange mixture of chlorine and ripe vegetation. Before the sun could broil our skin, we'd abandon our floats for the shallow end, tossing our bathing suits to the grass and submerging ourselves in the lukewarm water. Only our heads, wet hair plastered along the sides, would show.

Our laughter interspersed serious, whispered conversations about dreams, aspirations, and ideas for projects: a mural needing a wall, a book demanding an audience, or an art curriculum as the hub of a child's education. But mostly, nonsense and gossip eclipsed substantial philosophies. After all, it was summer in a Southern college town, a time to move slowly.

Now when I view photographs from that time—so many of them taken with color film, others in black and white and some colored by hand—I see myself as a teenager. Fresh-faced and long-limbed without an inch of fat, a bit stiff and awkward; certainly not a mom with kids at home. For those few hours, the responsibility I typically felt took a backseat. There were no arguments, worries, alarm clocks, or schedules. I enjoyed the carefree life I hadn't experienced during my childhood. At Kiki's pool, the sky was always cerulean blue and dotted with cotton candy clouds. Life was bliss.

On most days, Kiki held court from her floating chair equipped with a never-empty beer can holder. She sported spiked hair before it was fashionable and stood solid in her opinions. She bet five dollars that she and I were the same height. An easy back-to-back assessment showed the top of her head at my eye level. With a pout, a shake of her head, and hands firmly on her hips, she retorted, "Well, I *feel* like five-foot-seven."

When the shadows from the old oaks lengthened across the lawn, we gathered our things and said our goodbyes. Phyllis would drive to her ex's home to pick up their preschooler, and I'd be on my way in the opposite direction, often stopping for groceries. My boys would be at home with their dad, typically building Lego villages by the creek or riding bikes in the neighborhood. For the rest of the evening, the calm and serenity I felt at Kiki's pool stayed with me.

CHAPTER 4
The Wedding

ONE PARTICULAR DAY in early June, Kiki stood in the corner of the pool and shouted to us, "I have an announcement." She paused for emphasis and said it again.

Carole, with her large-brimmed floppy hat and pasty-white sunblock on her nose, plopped off her raft and splashed toward Kiki in the shallow end. The rest of us joined them. What could really be all that important?

With a flourish of her hand, Kiki pronounced, "We have a wedding date, August 3rd in Charleston."

Phyllis and Joan cried out in unison. "No! Absolutely not."

Kiki glared. In the silence, a few birds flitted in the nearby magnolia. A carpenter bee zoomed.

"Absolutely not," Joan said again.

"Absolutely not!" chimed Phyllis.

Kiki furrowed her brow, which made her eyes squint, and pressed her hands hard against her hips.

"Bad luck," said Joan and Phyllis in definitive unison.

"That date's bad luck," said Phyllis, and then her voice softened. "Joan and

I were both—do you believe *both*—married on August 3rd, and now we're divorced. Both—really, both—our husbands left us for other women they met at work. Both of us. Same situation, same wedding date. Don't do it. It's bad luck."

Joan, the most sensible one among us, vehemently nodded her consensus.

Kiki looked away and then back at the two women. Her hands were no longer on her hips, her voice sounded humbled. "Well, that's just silly, and anyhow it's too late. We have the church, the banquet hall, eight antique cars for the wedding party, and a band that's so popular most people have to book them a year in advance, but we got a deal."

I accepted Kiki's invitation to be a bridesmaid, and Joan and Phyllis stayed home, not wanting to contribute to the bad karma.

Eleven months after the wedding, Kiki's husband packed his clothes and books into his van, left his keys and a note on the dining table: *Sorry. You can keep the house.* He moved in with his mistress, a coworker.

The next month on August 3rd, we rallied to make sure Kiki's "anniversary" was unforgettable in the most positive way. The five of us arrived one-by-one around noon lugging tote bags bulging with presents, champagne, chocolate, cassettes tapes, cameras, camcorders, salads in Tupperware, containers of bubble-blowing soap, cigars, and a little pot. White lights dangled invisible in the bright sun and seventeen plastic pink flamingos surrounded the pool. Music from stereo towers, turned toward the backyard, filled all remaining space.

For the next six hours, we floated on our rafts and perched at the pool's edge gorging on strawberries, squirting first them and then ourselves with Reddi Whip. We laughed, sang, and mugged for Phyllis's always-ready camera.

Once twilight crept through the oaks outlining the property, we moved to the deck for dinner, champagne, and of course, wedding cake. For the past year, the top tier had waited patiently in the freezer for the newly married couple to once again place a morsel of cake into each other's mouths. Instead, the sugared trophy sat on a silver plate in the middle of sunburned, red-eyed friends who playfully leaned against each other, mostly to keep from falling off the deck's narrow benches. Kiki ceremoniously cut the cake as we toasted her resilience and our steadfast loyalty.

Then someone noticed we didn't have forks. Without missing a beat, Kiki scooped up a large piece of the cake with her hand. Icing squished through her fingers and smeared over her arm. We all followed suit, ending up with white goo-painted mouths and cake crumbs spewing like confetti.

Before long, night relegated the pink flamingos to the shadows. The strings of white lights twinkled like falling stars.

Sick of men, sick of their platitudes, we all related in our own way. As for me, I sensed that the ongoing, often subtle, conflict in my own marriage had become poisonous. I tried not to think about it and ate another hunk of cake.

We turned up the volume and danced until midnight, singing along to our new anthem about loving the nightlife and giving up on men.

CHAPTER 5

Generations

PHYLLIS AND I were more in sync with each other than we had ever been with the men in our lives. I believed my legacy of romantic malcontent was generational, punctuated early on by Grandma's continual declaration, "Men will disappoint you."

Grandma had left behind "true love" (her words) in Germany when her disapproving family offered her the ultimatum of working in a convent or finding a more promising husband in the States. She was nearing the end of her childbearing years, and most of all, wanted a family. Grandpa, also German but living in New York, was a widower and wanted a wife. Their lifelong marriage was one of convenience. They tolerated each other.

My mother married twice. Also disappointed, she gloried in the many years she spent unattached.

I wanted to prove them both wrong, but my rash decisions ended up supporting their experiences. Yet, instead of giving them credit, I attributed my missteps with men to my father's death when I was just two years old. I heard various accounts of that fateful event over and over again, but the primary elements were the same: late night thunderstorm, friend driving, crossing a bridge to New Jersey, collision with a truck, thrown from the car onto rain-soaked concrete, dead upon impact.

The 1:00 a.m. call had jolted Mom awake. Decades later, she'd say to me, "Calls in the middle of the night are never good news."

In the days after my father died, she packed up our things and bundled up her babies—my newborn brother and me—and left the small apartment she hated and her life as a housewife, which she also hated, and moved back into her parents' home on 43rd Avenue in Queens, New York. She was twenty-three years old.

My mother's younger sister, a storyteller, recounted the epilogue to the car accident many times. Referring to my mother after she'd returned to her parents' home, Auntie proclaimed, "She walked down the stairs wearing blue jeans and a blouse, red lipstick, and not a tear in her eye."

Mom went to work and became the family breadwinner. Her sister became our babysitter, Grandma became our mother, and Grandpa remained "Grandpa," a complicated man who rattled his newspaper while announcing headlines about murders and rapes.

Loss took up residency, nibbling away at my self-esteem, sometimes lounging in the background or lingering just behind my eyes so that they no longer sparkled. The same storyteller aunt would later rave about our wonderful childhood—the games, the books, all the art supplies—but then she'd footnote, "You were always a moody child."

She was right. I remember craving solitude, a time to sit with my special blanket and suck my thumb.

As young as four years old and throughout those early years, I'd search for a narrative within the thick black photo album, which lay heavy on my thighs. I'd turn page after page, mesmerized by the photographs, two by three inches, some with scalloped edges, some smooth. Faces and places stared at me, begging for words to define them. I imagined loving phrases between Grandma and Grandpa who stood rigidly in their winter coats on a Manhattan street. I assigned endearments to my father, the blond man with the wireframed glasses, holding me above his head. "Look how beautiful you are! There you go, there's that smile. There's my pretty little girl."

Grandma made sure we had vegetables fresh from the market each day, sensible shoes—no loafers, absolutely not—and bi-annual visits to the dentist. When I rode my bike or skated around the block, I knew she'd be there when I returned. I only needed a father.

Shortly before my tenth birthday, I thought my dreams had come true. Grandpa converted the upstairs of our house into an apartment. Mom was getting married. When I think back on that time everything blurs, and when I assign years to dates and dates to events, they don't compute. I remember secrecy—hushed voices in the kitchen—or no comments at all. No explanations. Just that Mom was getting married on January 15th without a wedding.

Our new family lived upstairs away from Grandma, who had been our mother for so many years. My new stepfather didn't speak much. He brought a mangy, growly dog with him—our previous pets had been sweet parakeets—and sat slouched on a straight-backed chair in the tiny kitchen. Even now, the only image I can conjure of him in those days is there at the table wearing suit pants, no belt, and a white undershirt.

My brother and I now shared a bedroom and were sent to Maine that summer. Wilderness Farm Camp for two city kids. Oh, the horrors of bringing in the cows! While we were away, our new baby brother was born.

Soon after, and this is where the dates get really confusing, we moved to Long Island. Perhaps this was the plan all along because my stepbrother and stepsister lived there with their mother, or maybe the good schools drew us. Perhaps Grandma's stare and crossed arms made my new stepfather nervous. In any case, we moved to Glen Head and into a cramped Cape Cod on a street with no traffic.

Mom relinquished her career for housekeeping. The mother I had known as someone wearing red lipstick and a sleek suit, the one who managed billing complaints from thousands of customers, now scowled and sighed anxiously as she fluttered around the kitchen trying to have the peas, potatoes, and chicken ready at the same time.

Most weekday afternoons, while the brother closest to my age routinely sequestered himself in his bedroom, I'd walk to the elementary school playground with my younger brother and a precious sister whom we later lost at the age of four. We'd return as dusk cloaked the neighborhood, and I'd peek into the window to see if my stepfather was stretched across his bed, snoring. When I thought it was safe—no embarrassing drunken behavior for the toddlers to witness—I'd sneak them into their room, whisper a bedtime story, and retreat upstairs to do my homework.

My bedroom, my refuge, was tucked under the slant of the roof. A "secret" door the size of a small window opened to the eaves where I hid journals filled with imagined romance.

Over the next eight years, I lived in that home with my blended family. I pined for a steady boyfriend to hold my hand, but my painful shyness kept me withdrawn. The simple act of talking to a boy was frightening because I had grown up without practice. No father, no good role model to take his place. My idealized view of boys didn't help, either. How could a teenager compare to Paul McCartney?

Yet girlfriends naturally gravitated to me. We found it easy to share secrets, outfits, and hairdryers. Our friendships were always dependable for a good laugh or a daring adventure.

CHAPTER 6

The Marietta House

MANY LIFE EVENTS later, and early on during a teaching career that would span thirteen years, I said to a colleague, "I believe teaching elementary school art is like playing professional football. It's not sustainable after you're forty years old—too physically and emotionally draining."

The idea had been planted, and soon after the August 3rd, twelve-hour celebration of Kiki's wedding anniversary, opportunities presented themselves. I was nearing forty and was, in fact, ready for a career change. I traded pool lounging for studying instructional systems in grad school while continuing to teach art. A new group of friends filled my days and evenings, even though Phyllis and the Dancing Girls remained like family, connected even though we spent less time together. And then there was Kiki, who interpreted my studies in a new direction as abandonment of her and the entire field of art education. She didn't speak to me for a year.

My marriage dissolved in 1986, the year I received my master's degree. True to form, Phyllis suggested we have a "Just Divorced Carport Sale."

"Well, people have moving sales and just married sales, why not a divorced sale?" she said, musing over her own divorce from the journalist years earlier. She placed the announcement in the Tallahassee Democrat.

On a sunny Saturday morning, we hung our wedding dresses—my mini and Phyllis's long satin one—from the trees bordering her driveway. Old mugs, dishware, clothes, and knick-knacks covered three folding card tables. We had a few customers and sold items for the amount they offered us. Some things we gave away. Mostly, we reminisced and drank strong Italian coffee. I felt content. Phyllis and the Dancing Girls—along with grad school friends— were an important part of my evolving life as a single woman.

A few years later, an intriguing man from my past, who had moved near Atlanta, revisited Tallahassee. He had been part of the local art community, an acquaintance in Phyllis's larger circle. We reconnected slowly, but eventually became a couple. One evening, I discovered a diamond ring resting in the bottom of my wine glass.

Phyllis was dating a fellow painter. "I've always had a boyfriend," she once said to me, and it was true. There was always a man in her house, and two or three waiting at the doorstep. Eventually the two artists married. The ceremony was glorious in full Dancing Girls tradition: cigars to smoke, bubble soap to blow through plastic wands, and of course, a dance floor.

A year later, great friends but not substantial spouses, the couple split. I decided that I would do just about anything to make my own romance work, even if it meant relocating from my beloved Tallahassee to my fiancé's home in Georgia. My sons were now in college, and I was determined to make the relationship a success.

But it wasn't.

A month before I was scheduled to move, I spent two weeks in his shot-gun house in the rural part of the state. "You need to try it out," he had said, "You've only been here on weekends." Yes, and during those weekends, we visited Virginia Highlands, an Atlanta tree-lined neighborhood of craftsmen bungalows with a vibrant crossroads of shops and bars, the place where I assumed we'd live.

I tried. I hung my things on the metal bar he put up for my closet. I ignored the rotting appliances and looked the other way when bathing in a tub sprouting rust like an infectious disease. At the end of two weeks, I told him his house was not for me. I'm sure I stumbled around with my words, but that was the message. I expected him to understand, I thought we'd discuss a solution, but he remained silent.

Before leaving town to pack the house in Tallahassee, which had recently sold, I stopped ten minutes from his place and rented an apartment. We could work it out. We had yet to choose a wedding date, and now I had a year's lease.

Once relocated, a routine fell into place. Weekdays, I lived in the one-bedroom apartment, developing training materials for social service agencies as an independent contractor. During the weekend, I stayed with my fiancé.

The apartment was cozy. When I finished work, before I turned on the gas fireplace, I'd sit on one of the two chairs positioned on the narrow balcony. Loss, which now included Tallahassee, my sons, and the Dancing Girls, sat in the other.

By the time the lease was up, I had accepted a full-time management position at Georgia Academy and Family Connection, a non-profit located in downtown Atlanta. That could change everything.

"Now I have a guaranteed salary. I can get a mortgage," I said to my fiancé. "What if I purchased a house for us? We could both commute, you to your house and studio, and me to the city."

He turned his back and walked away.

I ignored his silence—certainly he'd come around—and I found a real estate agent. When she and I pulled into the cul-de-sac at the bottom of a hill on Winding Creek Way in Marietta, Beethoven's "Ode to Joy" boomed majestically from the car radio. Surely a "sign."

A twenty-five-foot-high beamed ceiling and a huge stone fireplace dignified the living-dining area. The kitchen was large, sunshine yellow with an eating area by a bay window. A raised deck presided over a wooded lot that backed onto farm property for complete privacy. And the master suite by itself was more spacious than the downstairs of my entire childhood home.

He didn't show up at the closing. My gut knew then.

A week later, he loaded my things and the few pieces of furniture I had brought from Tallahassee into his pickup and moved them into the house on Winding Creek Way. The king-sized bed I had purchased for us had already been delivered. Then he backed up his truck in the turn-around area of the driveway, the part with the basketball goal, and put it into drive with enough gas for the tires to screech as he took off.

I sat cross-legged on the carpet in the middle of that big empty room with the high ceilings, a tiny speck in that cavernous space. Numb.

A month later, Phyllis arrived. She circled the rooms, waving her arms like windmills. "No art, there's no art. You need art; you must have some art. Of course, this is sad, very sad. We must hang some art."

The next month she visited again, this time with the Dancing Girls. She brought a painting large enough to almost cover one of the bare walls and a sculpture she called a "Sha-mama."

"I finished her skirt in the van while Kiki drove." Phyllis hummed into her words as she presented her creation assembled from a tomato cage, palm fronds, half a horseshoe crab (for the face), strips of burlap (the clothing), and mirrored scraps for eyes.

Phyllis leaned toward me. "Mystical powers," she said with a hush to her voice.

She moved the sculpture from the entryway to a corner of the large room, then over to the window, and back again to the entryway, all the time emphasizing, "Not a Shaman, a *Sha-mama*. Female, women power, our power."

Phyllis eventually positioned it by a chair. "She'll keep you company and help you heal, and . . . ." Her words trailed off into breath as she surveyed the house for the best wall to hang the painting.

Meanwhile, the others crammed champagne, cheese and fruit—vegetarian fare especially for Phyllis—into the refrigerator. Cabinet doors banged; drawers scraped open.

"What a great kitchen."

"Look how cozy it is by the window."

"I wonder if the morning light comes in on this side."

Kiki, who had finally forgiven me, rattled multiple strings of lights as she wove them through the railing on the deck. When fading sunrays filtered through the pines, we dragged out chairs. We drank champagne, munched on salads, and puffed very dainty cigars. Later, we went inside to dance. Ah, the large, empty space was good for something!

On Sunday afternoon, I stood at the end of the driveway by the mailbox and waved goodbye as Kiki's van wheeled up the hill.

On Monday, as usual, I met the commuter bus at the Cobb County Civic Center.

"Morning," the bus driver bellowed with a huge grin.

I took my seat as if it were assigned—third row from the back—and watched the car dealerships pass by in a gray blur on the way to my new position at the non-profit.

When we rounded Peachtree Street, my eyes widened, just as they did every Monday after a weekend in the suburbs. Downtown Atlanta was all abuzz with sunshine, bustle, and color. Business men and women dressed in suits. A rather large man proudly wearing lavender. Women decked in fuchsia and chartreuse. More brown faces than white. An international city.

Georgia Academy and Family Connection offices were located on the eighth floor of the Coastal States Building. We had grand dreams of lifting families and children from poverty through changes in perspectives and policy, and deeding decision-making to those most affected. Representatives from local and statewide groups met in our large conference space for training. Each session began with a statement of mission and principles much like the pledge of allegiance in a school room.

I bounced from one meeting to another, covered white boards with design and implementation plans, and radiated the excitement of possibility. We were a simpatico band of do-gooders who would use a foundation of data to create solutions and truly affect positive change.

Heady. Exhilarating.

Still, my old pal, Loss, remained in a back room of my psyche. I discovered the gym on the second floor and spent lunch hours on the Stairmaster farthest away from the others with my earphones blasting Hootie & the

Blowfish. The same tape played every day as I plodded along, step by step, attempting to dissolve the massive knot lodged in my heart.

At 6:11 p.m., I'd board bus 101, greet the regulars, and snuggle into a seat by the window. I'd soon re-enter my cave on Winding Creek Way, meditate, eat dinner, and write in my journal. At bedtime, I'd reach across the too big king-sized bed to the wall where I had taped a piece of notebook paper and cross off another day with an *X*. I could do this.

Over time, days slipped unnoticed into weeks and then months. I joined Unity Church, gleefully allowing myself to be consumed with workshops and Sunday gatherings that closed with the congregation holding hands and singing. I'd sway and croon as if I were on stage, filled with the warmth of the lyrics and my connection to the strangers next to me.

"You could have returned to Tallahassee and the Dancing Girls," one of my new friends said after hearing my story.

"No, I had just purchased a house. I would have lost a lot of money and I'm too practical with finances for that. Anyhow, I believe the Universe wanted me in Atlanta, although I'm not sure why, and damn, if He or She didn't have to use a man, my sorry-ass fiancé, to get me here."

CHAPTER 7

No Good Men

PERHAPS MY NEW position as an instructional design manager was my fate. It changed the trajectory of my life from small college town familiarity to wide-ranging urban horizons. A diverse group of co-workers and clients opened my eyes to new perspectives. I felt valued, needed, and that my skills were critical to the success of our work with children and families.

After a period of laudable results, the Academy broadened its scope from statewide to national. I flew to San Diego with two colleagues to deliver training and took the opportunity to stay for the weekend to explore the area—the zoo, art museum, and the marina—definitely something that Phyllis would do. She'd always extend field trips with students and travels with co-workers to have extra time, just for herself.

On Monday, I approached the skycap to discover a tower of luggage behind his stand and a crowd of people.

"Checking in," I said.

"Cancelled," he replied.

"Cancelled? What do you mean cancelled?"

"All flights east cancelled, ma'am. Big snowstorm, a blizzard in some parts."

"What? What am I supposed to do? I don't live here."

"Sorry ma'am, you can ask inside."

I lugged my bag through the automatic doors to find shoulder-to-shoulder patrons grumbling and pleading with grim-faced ticket agents. I joined the mass to learn there were no flights to Atlanta or the East Coast, no word as to when conditions would change, and heard repetitions of *I'm sorry you have nowhere to go, but there's nothing we can do about it.*

I moved to a group with blank expressions sitting on the floor against a side wall with coats, purses, and bags strewn about like a picnic gone awry. I glanced at my feet. They were adorned with simple shoes, not snow boots. At least I was wearing socks and had my trench coat with me.

I finally made it home, and over the next week, I retold the story many times to co-workers, the regulars on the bus, the guys at the gym, and my new friends at Unity Church.

"Thirty-six hours," I said with a bit of a shout and a wave of my arm. "Yep, it took me thirty-six hours to get home from California, and . . ." I'd pause to add drama, ". . . with almost every mode of transportation possible: plane, train, renegade cab, and by foot!"

My listeners would gasp, and I'd recount my journey: a flight to Indianapolis—"Closer to Atlanta, right?"—a few hours of sleep on an airport floor, attempts to open my frozen car door, a transit train to Midtown only to discover the buses to the suburbs weren't running.

"I dragged my suitcase up the walkway to the High Museum after buttoning my coat up to my neck. The lone person at the museum said, 'Sorry, no cabs, well, no real cabs. You could try this guy,' and he gave me a crumbled piece of paper with a number on it."

My listeners would lean toward me as I related my adventure riding in the backseat of a low-slung, gold-colored Caddy that looked like a dinosaur. "The driver, a stooped-over man with thick shoulders and hair coming out of his jaw like a scared cat, drove north on I-75 at twenty miles per hour, never skidding. When he reached my neighborhood, I insisted he drop me off at the top of the hill. I'd walk the rest of the way. I didn't want him to get stuck—not being able to drive that Caddy back up—and have to stay at my place."

We all laughed.

Once I wrapped up the details, the listeners typically commented, "Quite an adventure, unbelievable!" "You did it," or "You managed."

Yes indeed, I handled it. But this was a turning point.

The suburbs, I had realized, were not for me. Never again would I be stranded. Never again would I not have a neighbor or someone to call. I needed to move to a place with public transportation, and if it wasn't working for whatever reason, a snowstorm or something, I needed to be within walking distance of the basics: food, a pharmacy, a doctor. I needed a community, a family, even if they weren't blood related.

Three weeks later, I contacted my real estate agent and asked her to sell my house. Enough time had passed so I would make a small profit. I'd rent an apartment or a loft in Atlanta, in the city where I should have lived all along.

On Saturdays, I prepared the house on Winding Creek Way for a buyer, painting walls and cleaning baseboards late into the night. The boombox blasted blues. Around 1:00 a.m., I knew Phyllis would soon call, so I closed up the paint cans, washed the brushes, and settled across the king-sized bed, ready to catch up on our week.

"Just a minute," she said. "Let me turn off *Evening of Blues*."

I smiled as I heard her phone bang around and imagined her crossing the kitchen with her extra-long phone cord to shut off the plastic radio perched on the counter.

"I'm back," she'd chirp, and she'd describe her week in her whispery high-pitched voice.

On one particular late-night call, her demeanor grew passionate, her voice emphatic. "We need to plan our retirement. We're entering our fifties now. It's important to think ahead, and we can't depend on men. Look at me, two husbands down the tube, and even if I was still married, I couldn't count on either one of them. I just don't think there are any good men out there. Well, maybe, but not around us."

She laughed, obscuring the beginning of her next sentence. ". . . need to stick together. We must plan our retirement ourselves."

"The two of us, family," she continued. "Let's buy a house together by the beach."

An image flashed as her words sunk in. Phyllis and I are wearing wide-brimmed hats, large black sunglasses, shifts—not bathing suits—sitting in Adirondack chairs by the Gulf. Our legs, mottled with time and sun, are outstretched before us. Our hair, still long, is gray. A wisp of a breeze brushes our cheeks and gulls squawk, but otherwise it's quiet. The expansive sky and barely-moving-water breathe peace into the late afternoon. Serenity wraps around the two of us like an oversized shawl.

"Yes," I said. "Yes. What a great idea!" I could rent an apartment in Atlanta and, at the same time, purchase a house by the beach with Phyllis.

So that night in June 1996, with me in my furniture-empty house in Marietta and Phyllis in her cluttered cinderblock in Tallahassee, a pact was cemented. Our individual paths forever entwined, and we had no reason to believe we wouldn't grow old together.

CHAPTER 8

Hilda's Home

WE HAD A plan. Our roles were defined; Phyllis would do the legwork, and I'd visit her options on the short list. It made sense. She lived closest to the Florida coastal towns we had in mind, and I was busy selling my house and looking for a place intown.

New Smyrna Beach on the east coast of Florida was an option, but nothing panned out. Grayton Beach on the Florida Panhandle soon advanced to first place. We checked it out in early July 1996, but the cost of beachside houses far exceeded our budget.

We paused our search for a week during the 1996 international games hosted by my newly adopted city. Phyllis would never miss a global event, especially when it was within driving distance and she had a place to stay. We commuted from my house in the suburbs, leaving early in the morning and returning at dinnertime. Downtown Atlanta became our playground. We mingled with the crowds on the streets and public transit trains, toured the free art shows, delighted in the dance performances, and attended a volleyball match thanks to courtesy tickets from my friends at the gym.

On July 27th, the night of the bombing at Centennial Olympic Park, we sat in horror twelve inches from the TV screen, safe in my house in Marietta, marveling at our good fortune. We had left that very area only an hour before the explosion.

Rather than return to Tallahassee, Phyllis tacked another leg onto her trip, a camping adventure in the Georgia mountains with her new guy friend. We met him in a parking lot close to the route they would take north to their cabin.

"Hi, I'm Marc. That's Marc with a *c*," he said as he stretched out his hand to me. He appeared serious and confident in John Lennon glasses, but his nervous laugh confused that perception.

His stature reminded me of a declaration Phyllis had made years back to explain her rejection of a suitor I found attractive. "I like shorter, slightly-built men," she had said. "You can have the taller, muscular ones."

"Thanks for your generosity, Phyllis," I'd said, and we both laughed.

The next week my house sold, and I placed a deposit on a rental, a loft in a newly renovated building a few blocks from Centennial Olympic Park. It would be ready in a month. I felt liberated as I emptied the contents of closets and drawers into cardboard boxes. I was finally, really, moving on.

One night in the midst of my packing, Phyllis called with laughter and words tumbling together. "Apalachicola," she bubbled. "It's going to be the new Key West, an artist's paradise! And it's near St. George's Island. It's perfect, just perfect, for us."

I had been to Apalachicola when I lived in Tallahassee. All university students showed up there at one time or another to lounge on the weathered decks, slurp raw oysters, and guzzle beer while birds patiently—or not—waited for leftovers. I had shopped in the stores packed to the rafters with seafaring novelties. To this day, I cherish my plastic pink flamingo and wood-carved mermaids. Back then, I had never considered Apalachicola a place to establish roots, certainly not an area to own a house, but Phyllis's enthusiasm lured me in.

"Okay, let's take a look after I'm settled downtown in the loft."

The weekend after Labor Day, we drove in Phyllis's van from Tallahassee through small towns to the coast where we meandered southwestward. Crystal-blue water peeked through the wind-crippled scrub oaks, causing us to giggle and squirm with each sighting. The thrill of a new adventure gurgled inside us as we passed the barnacled shacks of Eastpoint and the turnoff to St George's Island. Thrill exploded into joy when we reached the great open expanse of the byway that would become the bridge to our destination. Sky, water, and tiny slivers of marsh. Only our van and the road. It didn't matter that each of us had previously traveled this path. We were now here together entering an orb of possibility.

As we drove on, the bridge stretched heaven bound with no visible descent. I held my breath until we reached the summit, and there, as if in a fairy tale, a miniature town sparkled in the distance. We wound our way toward it, passing marshes, gulls, and weekend fishermen. Soon the Gibson Inn greeted us, a restored turn-of-the-century hotel with first and second-story wraparound porches. "Welcome to Apalachicola," it seemed to say. "Come sit a spell."

We drove slowly through the community of wide streets and no traffic lights. The line of shops on Market Street reminded me of Main Street in Westerns: treeless, raised sidewalks, sleeping unleashed dogs. I expected hitching posts and troughs for horses.

Two blocks over, the whitewashed waterfront lay in stark contrast to my envisioned frontier town with its fishing boats, boarded-up brick warehouses, and one-story cinderblock buildings crusted with peeling paint. Through the van's opened windows, we breathed in the pervasive but not unpleasant stink of fish and marsh.

Phyllis turned to me, smiled, and navigated into a diagonal parking space near a narrow door marked "Real Estate."

"You'll love Kevin," she said. "He's really an actor but makes his money selling houses. He's been around for years and really knows this place."

Kevin, lanky with a swish of sandy hair across his forehead—too young to have been around for years—greeted us with a dashing grin. He wore sun-yellow pants and a blue checkered shirt, a look that complimented the setting.

The first house he showed us was located near the Gibson Inn on a street with trimmed lawns and low picket fences. A traditional floor plan: living room, kitchen, two bedrooms, and a porch. I liked the place, even though it was small. The unfinished attic had potential for an art studio, and I thought the house address, "250," to be a good omen: $2 + 5 + 0 = 7$, my lucky number.

Without much discussion, we moved on to the next house, over and down a block on Fourth Street. Kevin walked swiftly ahead of us to unlock the door, then returned to the sidewalk where we waited. "Take a look," he said with a bit of a bow and a sweep of his arm.

I followed Phyllis, who was soon out of sight, up the path. I noted patches of grass surviving despite the sand, the L-shaped rip in the screen door, and the white, wooden porch swing. I crossed the threshold, but then abruptly stopped, assaulted by musty, stale air as if an ancient trunk had just been opened. I inched forward despite a passing thought about my allergies and looked upward. The ceilings were high, perhaps sixteen feet. Dust particles danced in the streaks of sunlight filtering in through the open door.

I assessed my position as "the main thoroughfare," a wide foyer from the front to the back door, rooms on each side, ending with the kitchen. A tattered red velvet couch, turned on its end, leaned against the staircase before me.

I moved into the room on my left, imagining a long-ago scene: a formal mahogany dining table in the center and sconces with candles between the tall, narrow windows. In reality, the room was empty. Faded pink and gray flowered wallpaper hung in ridges like creped skin.

I crossed the foyer to the room on the right side and found it large, the size of two rooms, with a fireplace and a connecting doorway to a small side room perfect for a daybed and an afternoon nap.

I heard Phyllis's footsteps above me, creaking floorboards and rustling.

I continued on to the kitchen. Wood-paneled cabinets, Formica-topped counters, old appliances. I didn't see myself cooking in this place, too old, and a bit creepy. I glanced out the backdoor window and saw a jungle: cabbage palms, magnolias, and rampant crab grass.

Leaving the kitchen, I climbed the staircase to find a tiny bathroom off the landing and two bedrooms, one on each side. I poked my head into the room on the right to find Phyllis in deep concentration and obscured behind her 35mm. *Click-click, click-click . . .*

The other bedroom's layout mimicked the right-side, but its dimensions were much smaller. I imagined a child sleeping under the eaves looking out at the treetops, and then I saw her daydreaming, sitting on the window seat that faced the street. I soon returned to the stairs, glancing quickly at the cardboard boxes overflowing with drapery material crammed behind the stairwell, and proceeded downstairs and out the front door.

"Interesting," I said to Kevin.

He nodded, and we moved on to other topics: community theater, his favorite plays, and the pitfalls of mixing untrained with semi-professional actors. Kevin paused mid-sentence when the screen door slammed.

Whap!

We both looked up. Phyllis bounced toward us, crying out, "This is it!" She paused, grinned, and gasped for air before continuing. "My dreams. This is the house I keep seeing in my dreams, the house with all the rooms. Rooms that go in and out of each other."

She repeated herself again and again, becoming more animated with each iteration, swaying and gesturing with her long arms. Her 35mm camera thumped against her chest.

We watched her, entranced. I smiled back, but because I was so surprised by her energy, I didn't know what to say. Phyllis literally glowed.

"This is it," she said again.

When she stopped for breath, Kevin told her the woman who owned the house had died there. "She was ninety-two years old, and I think she died in her sleep. She wasn't seriously ill, just old. I know she didn't go to a hospital. Yes, for sure, she died in that house."

Phyllis leaned in, her arms now motionless at her sides. "Really?"

"Yeah. There are relatives up north someplace, maybe Chicago, a son, I think. I don't remember. Anyhow, they don't want the house."

"I wonder why not," said Phyllis more to herself than to Kevin.

I remained silent, only partially listening, more captivated by the quiet. No traffic, no passersby, just a breeze sashaying through the tiniest of leaves and birds calling to each other. This part of town had lush foliage and farther down the block, large oaks formed canopies over the road.

Kevin continued, "She was quite a character, that Hilda, a fixture here in Apalachicola," He brushed his hair from his eyes. "Yep, Hilda Dunn. I didn't know her, but I saw her, like everyone else did, walking around town or down 98 to the grocery. She always had a netted bag slung over her shoulder to carry her purchases."

I perked up, turning my attention back to the conversation.

"She had long—really long—gray hair. I'm guessing it was once dark. And olive-toned skin, a strong nose. Her clothes were colorful, long skirts and vests upon vests . . ."

I no longer heard Kevin's words as I stared at Phyllis and saw her as an older woman. Hilda. She would look like Hilda. Perhaps when Hilda was young, she looked like Phyllis.

Oh my, and what about Phyllis's dreams? What's going on here?

Phyllis turned from Kevin to me. Her eyes appeared larger than ever. Her expression was serious. The pause between us was huge and heavy.

Eventually, she spoke. "What do you think?"

I didn't respond. I wasn't sure what I was thinking or feeling. Phyllis's entire countenance pleaded for an answer. I grasped for rationale. Is this an omen? Hilda, a prophecy? A foreshadowing of Phyllis at ninety-two? A sign that yes, this is the house for us to grow old in together, a place for our retirement? A home for our not-yet-born grandchildren to visit?

For a minute, I focused on the worn sandals I was wearing. I needed new ones. I felt Kevin standing to the side of us and sensed a calm neutrality about him. I looked up at Phyllis and met those eyes, which seemed to say *please, please, please* . . .

I cleared my throat, shuffled my feet, and then nodded. "Sure," I said.

Phyllis lunged at me, flipping her 35 mm to the side, and she wrapped her arms around me. She pulled back, gripped my hands, and grinned and giggled. As she laughed, her hair tossed around her shoulders.

And then, looking directly at me, she paused and called me *sister*.

CHAPTER 9

Co-owners

THE NEXT DAY as I drove north on I-75, a pervasive feeling of doubt invaded my thoughts. The house on Fourth Street was not what I expected: too dilapidated and too close to businesses. But the process of purchasing it was in motion. I had said *yes*. How could I change that? It was far easier to focus on whatever I could do to make it a place that would work for me. Redecorating ideas swirled in my mind as I passed the rural towns of middle Georgia: a remodeled kitchen, an updated screened porch, a landscaped yard. I assumed Phyllis would think my plans were as fabulous and necessary as I did.

Everything had been decided. I would take the smaller bedroom to the left of the stair landing, the one where I had imagined the girl daydreaming. Phyllis would take the larger bedroom on the right. The downstairs room, where I had pictured the mahogany dining table with the sconces between the windows, would serve as our joint art studio. I only needed Phyllis to agree to the improvements.

By the time I neared the I-285 loop around Atlanta, the incessant hum of my Nissan's engine had lulled my discontent into acceptance. Hilda's home would be ours. We'd be co-owners, and Phyllis would research mortgage possibilities.

Certainly we'd qualify.

Phyllis wasn't currently teaching full-time, but she had sufficient income from selling art and giving private lessons. Her Tallahassee house was almost paid off, and she had a good amount of cash savings. I didn't have that, but I had a salaried position and a small profit from the sale of the Marietta house. Both our names would be on the loan.

Once home, I unlocked the door to my loft apartment and smiled as I breathed in the pleasurable aroma of the floral arrangement sitting on the shelves in the foyer. A slight turn to the right took me to a long hall with a checkerboard linoleum floor and white walls, perfect for an art gallery. Paintings from my collection were stacked nearby waiting for someone with a ladder to help me hang them.

I walked past the two bedrooms with unpacked boxes still crammed into the corners, and entered the largest room, a true loft space with planked wood floors and a ceiling at least two stories high with exposed ductwork. The windows, three before me and two to the right, were enormous, appropriate for the building's original business, Muse's Clothing Company, circa 1874.

I plopped down onto my marshmallow of a couch and stretched out my legs across the top of a matching ottoman, and simply stared, exhausted. My ears filled with the cacophony of city sounds, the drone of the evening commute mixed with the sirens of emergency vehicles.

Before long, the phone rang. "Hey," my new neighbor-friend said. "You're back. Come over for wine. Let's catch up."

The following week, Phyllis crisscrossed the wide streets of Apalachicola with head-down determination in pursuit of a loan: bank, mortgage company, bank again, post office.

"Do you believe a U.S. Post Office closes for lunch?" she exclaimed.

Phyllis's laid-back disposition became more frantic as bankers negotiated. I received ongoing updates. We were joint owners. We weren't. She qualified.

Then she didn't. Yes. No. No again, but then yes.

Late one night when Phyllis called, her voice was so soft, I had to ask her to speak up and repeat herself.

"I don't qualify," she said with resignation. "They won't give me a loan because I don't have a real job."

"What? You have assets: the equity in your Tallahassee house, your—"

"Nope, I don't qualify." She paused. "But they'll give *you* a loan. By yourself."

Two weeks later, I left Atlanta at 6:00 a.m. in a rush to make it to the 1:00 p.m. closing. Phyllis greeted me outside the attorney's office, sidling up to me so our faces almost touched. I breathed in her scent, lemon and lavender.

"I need to talk with you before we go in," she whispered. "This is very important, very important to me." She paused for a second, glancing away. "I want to be on the mortgage papers," she said emphatically. "And I've figured out a way."

I looked at her face, somber and unflinching. I couldn't imagine what she had in mind.

"If we were sisters . . ." Her voice trailed off. "If we were sisters, then my name could be on the mortgage papers too." She took an audible breath.

Without thought—logic had been eclipsed by sentiment—I replied, "But we *are* sisters, aren't we?"

And with that, we walked into a small, rather dark office, lined with floor-to-ceiling bookshelves. The closing attorney greeted us with a homey warmth that reminded me of a mom who baked cookies and led Girl Scout troops. We took our places—Phyllis's chair right up against mine—at a polished cherry-wood table covered with organized piles of documents.

"Congratulations to the two of you," the attorney said. "I understand you're sisters. I can see the resemblance."

I turned to Phyllis who returned my questioning glance with a shrug, a tilt of her head, and an expression that said, *I knew you'd agree.* I found Phyllis's surety and our soon-to-be "legally" confirmed sisterhood endearing, and also, amusing.

As if choreographing a dance, the attorney stepped us through each line of the mortgage documents, confirming the location, loan amount, and the places needing signatures or initials. Phyllis signed her name underneath mine.

We left as homeowners. Arm-in-arm and sometimes bumping against each other, we walked to one of the town benches because Phyllis had something urgent to show me. She rumbled around in her cloth bag. "It's here someplace."

I waited. Her tote bulged and bunched as she searched. "I know it's here. I purposefully brought it to the closing . . . look! Ta dah!"

She waved a four-by-six-inch photograph like a flag and handed it to me. "It's Hilda. Hilda! She's still in our house. This is proof."

I studied the image: a window-like rectangle with a ball of light in its center shaped like a bird, and another streak of light, dusty and diffused.

"Well, these light patterns happen all the time with the last frame on a roll of film," I said.

"I know," said Phyllis. "At first, I thought that too, so I checked. This was *not* the last frame."

I wasn't convinced but nodded anyway; Phyllis beamed.

The deal was sealed. We had our retirement home, a place where our future grandchildren could visit, and where we'd wile away our hours painting large canvases as Delta blues bawled from the public radio station. The Dancing Girls would have open invitations because Phyllis and I expected to fill the house with kindred spirits.

Now I just had to get the furniture I had stored in the garage of the Marietta house, courtesy of the new owner, to Apalachicola. Phyllis's friend, Matt, a trucker, was moving freight from Columbus, Ohio, to West Palm Beach, Florida and agreed to add my belongings to his haul. The plan was for us to meet at the nearby civic center.

When I arrived, I gasped. The rig seemed to span half the parking lot! Standing by the cab at the far end, the driver appeared diminutive, even though in reality he stood over six feet. Matt, with his shaggy blond hair and surfer-boy grin, welcomed me to the trucker world.

I estimated it would take an hour to load my things; it took four. At
10:00 p.m., I grabbed the sidebars and pulled myself up and into the cab,
high off the pavement. Matt navigated to I-75 south, accelerating into a star-
less night amid the sounds of Led Zeppelin wailing from the tape player. I
stared out the window at the roofs of cars as we rumbled past them, buzzing
with excitement and disbelief that I was rollin' down the highway in an eigh-
teen-wheeler, queen of the road.

At 1:00 a.m. we pulled into a Flying J truck stop to get some sleep. I
soon found myself strutting, still queen of the road, through aisles of trucker
accessories to the ladies' room under the watchful eye of a gray-shirted sheriff.

When I returned to the rig, Matt signaled for me to take the berth behind
him, a nest he had made with blankets. A dreamcatcher bobbed over my head.

I cascaded into a heavy, dreamless sleep, and even when the big engine
eventually started again, I didn't budge, snuggled and rocked as if I were in a
pram. Hours later when sun and heat seared through the window, I kicked off
my blankets and slowly opened my eyes. Florida! Only a couple more hours
to Apalachicola and my new second home.

I climbed over the seat and kissed Matt on the cheek, "Good morning."

He smiled. "There's a thermos of coffee on the floorboard . . . with cream."
Ah, he remembered from one of our phone conversations.

When we arrived at Fourth Street, Matt positioned the truck as close
to the property as he could, but the rig still dominated most of the street. I
expected Phyllis to burst from the screened porch—I could almost hear the
door squeak and slam—but all was quiet.

I turned to Matt, "I wonder where Phyllis is. I wanted her to see me up
here in this cab. What a hoot. She'd love it."

We took our time disembarking. Matt inspected the tires and unloaded
my furniture. I gathered my suitcase and tote bags. Still, no Phyllis. Certainly
she heard us.

I walked up the path and into our unlocked home. My footsteps resound-
ed as I walked through the foyer past the side rooms to the kitchen, all empty.

I opened the back door with a crunch and discovered a scene from *Under the Tuscan Sun*: a haphazard garden, guests sitting around a spool table, mismatched folding chairs, pastries, coffee, and chianti in its straw wrap with jelly jars for glasses.

"Phyllis," I shouted as I leaped down the cement steps.

She rushed toward me, her metal chair tumbling to the grass.

The others remained seated: an older couple I recognized from a previous visit as our neighbors from across the alley, and Marc.

What was Marc doing at our house? Marc with a *c*. Marc with the nervous chuckle.

Our initial meeting at the parking lot in Atlanta three months ago flashed through my memory: he and Phyllis giggling, locking eyes, brushing shoulders. I should have known then. They're a couple—more of a couple than I had thought—a couple in *my* house.

Suddenly, the second thoughts I'd been having about the house—the extent of needed maintenance and renovation, the six-hour drive, the mega gas station being built on the corner—felt more consequential.

CHAPTER 10

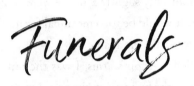

BACK WHEN I was teaching art in Tallahassee and spending summers at Kiki's pool, before grad school and before Atlanta, grocery shopping took hours. Inevitably, I'd run into parents or other teachers and engage in lively conversations.

One evening in 1983, I had bumped into an acquaintance, the drama teacher from a private school. He looked haggard and drained; understandably, as I discovered he had recently accompanied eighth graders to the funeral for one of their classmates.

"I don't believe in funerals," I said, leaning on my grocery cart. Up until this conversation, I had shunned anything traditional, whether it was organized religion or corporate America. After all, I was a product of the 60s.

When my teacher-friend heard this, he moved his grocery cart to the side. In his booming bass voice and with eloquent gestures, very much the drama teacher, he emphasized, "It's the very first step in healing. Funerals are ceremonial. Think of all the civilizations throughout time. They've all had rituals."

He continued to expound, naming several cultures and describing their rites of passage: birth, coming of age, marriage, and death. Shoppers maneuvered around us. Drops of moisture ran down the sides of the milk container in my cart.

His words were convincing and made me think of my sister Laurie's funeral. I didn't think that was healing at all. Her casket—white, the size of a four-year-old girl, a spray of pink roses on top—was still clear in my mind's eye.

Her illness, a brain tumor, had traumatized our family. When Laurie's symptoms significantly advanced, Mom placed her in a crib next to her bed with the bedroom door only slightly ajar. We weren't allowed to visit. I supposed Mom thought it would be too emotional for us. Our baby sister could no longer walk and wore diapers again.

When Laurie died in Mom's arms, I was the only other person in the house, so I believe I was the first person she told. I was fifteen years old. I don't remember what Mom said, only that she added, "I've called the Montforts. You can go there for dinner."

My friend's family ate a formal meal in their dining room. I had artichokes dipped in butter for the first time.

The funeral took place on a sunny day at a steepled church with arched stained-glass windows and a large cross over the oak doors. Budding tulips and daffodils lined the walkways. We sat in the second pew reserved for the family: Mom, my stepfather, and I assume my other siblings, but I have no recollection. I didn't see anything, only that casket. That tiny, white, flower-draped box with Laurie's little girl body inside. My pooling tears became great, loud sobs. My chest heaved and I gasped for air like a poor, sad, floundering fish. In that hush-quiet church, I felt someone's hands on my shoulders maneuvering me from the pew, down the aisle, and through the oak doors. Outside, I stopped crying. I could breathe again. I would soon hear adults talking around me, but not to me, deciding that someone—I don't remember who—needed to take me home. I definitely could not go to the cemetery, they said.

It would be forty years before I attended another funeral.

In the Fall of 1999, Annie, one of the Dancing Girls, called me in Atlanta to say Maxi, Phyllis's father, had died.

Maxi, short for Maximillian, had hailed from Sicily. An artist himself, his appearance reminded me of the surrealist, Salvador Dali. It wasn't unusual for Phyllis and her father to participate in the same art show.

I remember sitting at Phyllis's kitchen table on more than one occasion when the door from the carport would burst open and Maxi's energy entered the house before his body. He'd move swiftly through all the rooms with his furrowed brow and determined walk, then encircle them again, calling *Phill*-us, *Phill*-us, ignoring me and anyone else who was there.

Phyllis and Maxi were close; I felt for her. Of course I would attend her father's funeral, even though she and I hadn't communicated for the past several months. I had pulled out of our partnership two years after we signed the mortgage papers. I viewed the dissolution as business; Phyllis saw it as divorce.

I had my reasons. Downtown Atlanta had shifted my priorities and opened my eyes to a vibrant urban world, the distinct opposite from a town without a traffic light.

On a typical day, I might chat with U.S. Congressman John Lewis in the Starbucks coffee line or pass social activist Julian Bond strolling by the old Macy's. One morning, I discovered a black-coated, sunglass-wearing, ear-pieced Secret Service agent at our loft entrance, because President Bill Clinton was speaking in the park across the street.

I had become accustomed to places like the bar at the Ritz where men with skin the color of onyx and amber sipped whiskey, jostled each other, and smiled at women. Parades seemed to be spontaneous, art festivals omnipresent, and getting to the stage to hear Ray Charles sing "Georgia on My Mind" was an easy walk from my loft.

Apalachicola was the polar opposite. In the raw oyster bars overlooking the bay, I sat next to residents, tourists, and college students: all white, no people of color. During one particular visit, I ambled into a luncheonette for coffee. A typical eatery: pale yellow walls covered with lattice work, daisies in clear glass vases, groups of two and three women seated at round tables. While sipping my latte, I observed a Black man walk to the counter, order and wait, standing, as his food was prepared. Then he picked up his Styrofoam container in a plastic bag, retraced his steps, and left. Why didn't he sit down, or eat in? Was I reading more into this than the situation implied? Nevertheless, it made me question my decision. Did I really want to own property here?

And then there was Marc. I wanted to say something to Phyllis, something like: *We purchased this house because we had given up on men, right? Now Marc is here and sleeps with you in the bedroom across the hall from mine.*

But I didn't.

It could have been a spell arranged by Hilda, who continued to let us know she was still with us. Doors randomly closed, Phyllis's kimono somehow got snared into the wall, and clothes moved from one end of the closet to the other. I don't think Hilda ever liked me—I believe she knew I wanted the other house, the renovated one down the street—and she used me. My salaried job was necessary for a mortgage loan to get Phyllis, the daughter she never had, to inherit the home she had loved for a lifetime. That's what I believed, anyway.

I researched real estate comps and created a buyout plan before approaching Phyllis. In the past two years, the property had almost doubled in value. Phyllis now had a full-time teaching job, so she could get her own mortgage loan and buy out my share or we could sell and split the profit.

When I laid out the options, the color drained from Phyllis's face, her eyes dulled, and her shoulders collapsed. We negotiated. For three months. Letters to and from Atlanta: Phyllis's were handwritten, often in pencil with text seeping into the margins and circling the page, while mine were computer-typed.

Phyllis: This was to be our home; not a business deal.

Me: My interest has changed. There's always change in relationships. That's why we talked through all the possibilities beforehand. Remember that trust agreement?

Phyllis: Friends, lenders, and realtors say that since you're pulling out, you're lucky not to be taking a loss. (Someone must have told her this, because those were not words she would say!)

Me: I don't understand. Each of us has always had the right to pull out. We agreed to that upfront. Are you talking about money or a broken promise? If this is about our personal pledge, then for that I sincerely apologize and hope that one day you'll understand.

The back and forth continued. I'd decipher Phyllis's letters, sometimes written on pages of sketchbook paper, and return a bulleted list to her. "You said *bullet, bullet, bullet*. We agree on *this* and *that*. I offer *bullet, bullet, bullet*." I consulted a real estate lawyer. More letters, more back and forth.

We finally agreed. Phyllis would refinance the house in her name, send me a check for most of our agreed-upon amount, and then she'd follow-up with monthly payments.

Her initial check arrived with a note. Around the image of Miss Piggy writing valentines with a quill pen, Phyllis wrote,

"New home, new living arrangements, new jobs, old friends. Please wait until Friday before cashing. Thanks."

And that was that. We went on to live separate lives with no interaction. Her father's funeral was my opportunity to reconnect. I packed my suitcase, selecting a little black dress too sophisticated for Tallahassee, perhaps a statement to my urban-ness, and drove south on I-75 without notifying anyone of my intentions. I wasn't sure of the reception I'd receive.

At Bevis Funeral Home, I awaited my turn to greet the family: Phyllis; her mother, Violet; and her brother, Vince. Once the person before me in the reception line moved on, I faced them all.

Violet glared and her eyebrows lifted in astonishment. A small sound, not quite a word, escaped from her lips. Phyllis, standing next to her, gasped and opened her mouth wide as if to shout, but then simply grinned. The last in the receiving line, Vince, who always saw the irony of things, nodded and smiled with a glint in his eyes.

Years later, I would learn that Violet hated me for "what I did to Phyllis . . . making Phyllis pay all that money for her own house."

"What?" I replied to the person telling me this. "Technically, it was *my* house. I was the true mortgage holder."

But at the time of Maxi's funeral, I didn't know that. I just thought Violet was being her ornery self.

Moving into the chapel from the receiving line, I discovered the pews dotted with white origami doves. "My students made them," whispered Kiki as I squeezed in next to her.

On the altar was a ceramic urn created by a local artist. Phyllis's and her father's paintings were displayed on easels. An uncle spoke, as did Vince, and we all recited the Lord's Prayer.

Then silence.

We sat there for a few minutes, shifting in our seats, until the staticky, scratchy sound of an old record filled the room with a very familiar voice. Frank Sinatra. I turned to Kiki, dumbfounded. Muffled laughter filled the chapel. "That's Life" crooned ol' Blue Eyes. We imagined Maxi singing along with him, telling us he was rolling himself into a big ball . . . We knew the ending. My, my. We tossed the paper doves into the air.

I stayed in Tallahassee an extra day once everyone else left, believing that the day after the funeral would be tough for my friend. Phyllis was Daddy's Girl, and they were fellow artists. He always had something to discuss with her, just the two of them. Now he was gone.

I showed up at her Tallahassee home with chianti and plastic cups. Phyllis gathered cigars, matches, and cushions. We climbed the ladder in her art studio to the loft above it, and then squeezed through the window to the eaves as dusk slipped around us like a gauzy curtain. We leaned against the house and stretched our legs across the shingles. Phyllis poured the wine.

I picked up my cup. "Let's toast Maxi."

Phyllis smiled, nodded, and lifted hers now brimming with chianti. She turned toward me, her voice breaking with laugher, "Yes, yes. I think his soul is soaring now. Somewhere over Miami or Sicily."

I offered my drink to the heavens. "To Maxi, Phyllis's father."

We both sipped the warm, rich, slightly sour liquid.

"To the prolific self-taught artist," Phyllis chimed in. "To the lover of my cannoli," she shouted.

"To the man of elaborate eccentricities," I cried out, stumbling over the words.

"To the man who never wrote my name the same way twice," giggled Phyllis.

"Really?" I asked.

"Yes," and she spelled out *Fill-us, Phil-us,* and *Philll-us.*

I took another sip of wine and proclaimed, "To the man who ignored everyone else except his lovely, darling daughter."

Phyllis murmured; her shoulders shimmied with delight.

"To the crazy guy," we said in unison, taking large gulps of wine, residue dribbling down our chins.

"How 'bout a cigar?" asked Phyllis, looking around for the package. She got up on one knee, lost her balance, and skidded with a gravelly crunch across the asphalt and fiberglass that covered the eaves.

"Whoa! Look out." I grabbed her arm.

"I'm fine," she said with an uneven chuckle.

I maintained my grip until we were once again positioned on our cushions. We settled into silence and watched the smoke from our cigars swirl and dissipate into the night. A crescent moon smiled shyly in the sky. Crickets rolled their castanets.

The next morning, I stopped by before heading north on I-75. I looked over at Phyllis as I started the car. She stood in her front yard by the fern garden holding up two fingers. Peace. For the first time, I recognized the sadness I had been harboring since we had dissolved our plans to live together. It disappeared with Phyllis's simple gesture.

Ten months later and a few days into 2000, downtown Atlanta felt slow-moving like the morning after a raucous party. I stopped to pick up dinner at Jalissa's, a little hole-in-the-wall restaurant on Broad Street behind my loft. The Jamaican behind the counter put my order in as soon as he saw me walk through the door. I smiled at him and, without thinking, tossed my long hair with a shake of my head. I love this neighborhood and city life!

Back in my loft standing against the counter, I dug into the plantains, beans, and yellow rice. The soothing jazzy stanzas of the CD I had slipped into the player—*Maxwell's Urban Hang Suite*—filled the wide-open space and seemed to float up to the open ductwork.

The jarring ring of the phone crashed my composure.

Kiki. It was Kiki. I couldn't remember the last time she had called me or I had called her. We had caught up at Maxi's funeral, but we weren't phone chatters. Tonight, she talked about her classes, complained about the school administration, and rattled on about local politics. I filled her pauses with *umm* and *uh-huh*, wondering about the purpose of her ramblings while I finished my dinner.

Eventually, she said with an emphatic tone, "Phyllis awoke at 2:00 a.m. on the couch still wearing her coat and with her purse and tote bag by her side."

"What?" I was confused. Where did this come from? Was this about school and Phyllis's heavy schedule of classes?

Kiki's words sped up; one sentence fell into another until I expected her to begin panting.

"I've been worried about Phyllis. She seems so tired lately. Dragging. And she has these big bags under her eyes. Dizzy too. We both thought she needed extra vitamins. There's been a lot going on. You know, the holidays. Art classes and kids are crazy. Then this 2:00 a.m. thing, waking up on the couch. She must have walked in the door after school, sat down and that was it. No dinner. Sound asleep. Until 2:00 a.m. I think that worried her too. She told me her annual physical was scheduled for mid-January, but she wanted to move it up. She called and they took her, but it was New Year's Eve. Everyone closing early. Her doctor wasn't working, but Phyllis saw her assistant."

My shoulders tensed. Why all these details? *Get to the point, get to the point.*

But Kiki continued to chatter at a frantic pace. "And then the very next day—how often does that happen? —the doctor's office called. New Year's Day. Most places are closed, you know. They had Phyllis come in. They said something about talking to her about her bloodwork. Anyhow, it wasn't good. When Phyllis arrived at the office, her doctor was there—not the assistant—her doctor of many years."

Kiki took a breath that ended with a drawn-out sigh, and I realized I was holding mine.

"Phyllis has cancer," Kiki said. "Multiple myeloma," she said. "Terminal cancer."

CHAPTER 11

I-15 Back and Forth

I COLLAPSED INTO my soft-pillowed club chair. Numb. Paralyzed. Evening faded into night. Patterns of light from the streetlamps climbed the loft's walls and wound themselves around the ceiling's pipes like untamed vines.

I hiked up my knees, pulled them toward my chest, and wrapped my arms around my legs. My ball of protection against a cruel set of circumstances, the same position I held when I awaited my four-year-old sister's diagnosis. Brain tumor, inoperable. And now Phyllis, multiple myeloma, terminal.

Tears spilled onto my cheeks, a steady roll of anguish with a mind of its own. Heaving and sobbing didn't occur until much later, when I finally managed to extricate myself from that chair and toddle, ever so slowly, to the bedroom. There, open and exposed, lying in the center of a king bed, I fixated on the ceiling twenty feet above me and wept. Grief had claimed me.

My initial thought was to immediately drive to Phyllis's home, a five-hour trip, but I quickly rejected the idea. Driving at night meant frightening uncertainty. Darkness, pierced only by my headlights along dim highways with trucks whizzing by me. Shrouded rural roads.

I couldn't do it.

"Call her," Kiki had said, "but wait a couple of days. She's in the hospital getting a shunt so she can take her chemo at home."

So I waited. I sought solace in my routines: morning and evening meditation, journal-writing, fusion dance classes, and my latest contract gig, now that I had left my salaried position and was working on my own from a home office. I savored coffee with neighbors, walks with women friends, and workouts around Centennial Olympic Park with my guy friend. But sadness remained inside me like a dull ache made worse by distance and my imagination, which colored my dear friend with horrendous sickness and death.

When I finally reached Phyllis, I was pleasantly shocked to hear her breathy voice sprinkled with laughter. "How are you?" she asked.

"How am *I*? You're the one who . . ." I couldn't finish that sentence.

The typical clamor of chaos in Phyllis's kitchen—dishes clanging, chairs scraping, Marc and Vince's raised voices—threatened to obscure our conversation.

"I'll drive to Tallahassee tomorrow," I shouted.

"No," Phyllis replied emphatically. "Wait until after I have my first round of chemo. They say I'm going to have a good period. That's when I'd like you to visit, not when I'm feeling bad. I don't want you here while I'm sleeping or vomiting or whatever happens."

My Tallahassee trip wouldn't be for three weeks.

While sitting at Starbucks, a neighbor exclaimed, "You're waiting three weeks to visit your best friend after hearing she has terminal cancer? That's really hard to believe. If it were me, I'd have the car keys in hand as I hung up the phone."

She snorted and hmphed, leaving me sufficiently shamed and blubbering excuses. "But Phyllis told me not to come. She was very specific."

My solution was to stay connected by calling every other day. Sometimes I'd talk to her answering machine or to her brother, Vince, but mostly, she answered, even though we often only spoke for a few minutes. Before long, I discovered piles of notes on scrap paper, my incessant scribbling as I listened to her words.

One note read:

> Having chemo is like going to jail. Especially with
> Dr. Gloom and Doom.

Another on the back of an envelope read:

> Tired, just so tired. I try to do things, I can't.
> So much to do. Stuff all over the place.
> The Christmas tree is still up. Oh! Haircut
> appointment! ! !

Still another note:

> I have a boy's haircut, nothing in the back!
> Never knew how much your hair keeps you warm.
> Wish it was a little longer. I look like Ringo Starr.

At last, on a dazzling sunny day, warm for the end of January, I wheeled a suitcase to my building's parking deck shouldering two large tote bags brimming with project materials: photographs, magazines, matte medium. The valet greeted me with his gracious smile and pleasantries.

I was soon weaving my way south through downtown Atlanta to I-75. This would be the first of many long weekend trips, which over time, developed into a rhythm: cassette music tapes, particularly Willie Nelson and Linda Ronstadt—good singing and driving tunes—and audio books, at least one for each leg of the trip.

On this first visit, I was filled with angst. What would Phyllis look like? Would I need to care for her, and if so, *how*? I squirm at the sight of blood and wretch when someone vomits. What would we talk about? What should I say to someone with terminal cancer?

My nerves tensed as I came closer to the Georgia-Florida line. The sign,

"Welcome to Florida"—with a sun for the *o*—greeted me like a sentry. I turned off the cassette player. In the quiet, I could fully experience the sentimentality I felt driving along Tallahassee roads: streets that led to the home where I'd raised my sons, places I'd worked and studied, neighborhoods that housed a community I called "family," not of blood but of grateful choosing.

I pulled into Phyllis's driveway. Her cinderblock house, which was covered with pink stucco, stood quiet among the palms and ferns. I walked up the flagstone path, parting a curtain of thick, humid Florida air with each step. I very deliberately placed one foot after the other on each flagstone to ground and calm myself.

The door flew open, and there was Phyllis, smiling, radiant, and looking as if she had just stepped out of a shower. An indigo scarf was wrapped around her head, topped with a crocheted hat decorated in an Aztec pattern. Feathered earrings tickled the sides of her full cheeks—the result of steroids, I assumed.

We greeted each other with laughter instead of words until Phyllis said, "Come in, come in. Talk to Mom—she's in the kitchen—while I finish dressing."

I nuzzled and petted Spotless, Phyllis's Dalmatian, as I walked through the living room and the dining area to the kitchen where Violet sat at the end of the table facing me. A pang of the usual intimidation stabbed my confidence. Violet always reminded me of the hunched and sour woman in fairy tales, and here she was, staring, unsmiling, and wearing an imposing, dark coat buttoned up to her neck. A purse dangled from her arm. Tentatively, I pulled out the chair across from her and sat down.

Phyllis's kitchen served as the hub of household activity. Friends and family alike entered without knocking through the carport door or through the front door like I did. They leaned against the counter, which ran the length of one side of the kitchen, or freely opened the fridge that was covered with memorabilia and painted with an oversized sunflower to cover a brown spot. They might sit on one of the stools after shooing off a cat or select one of the mismatched wooden chairs surrounding the table. Inevitably, they'd stay put and never wander to other parts of the house.

I fiddled with the car keys I still had in my lap before looking up at Violet. "How are you? Are you enjoying your place by the river?"

Violet shrugged so deeply that her shoulders reached her ears, and she muttered something I couldn't decipher.

How in the world would I make conversation with this woman?

I took a purposeful breath before continuing.

"It must be nice out there," I said.

I shifted in my seat and noticed the heavy, smoky aroma of leftover coffee grinds. I wondered about excusing myself to use the restroom when I heard a low growling sound that appeared to come from the back of Violet's throat. She clasped her hands together on the table and craned her neck toward me.

"No one is telling me anything," she said firmly. "No one is answering my questions."

I winced, not expecting the force of her declaration, and then responded. "I think they're trying to protect you."

"I don't need to be protected." Her clutched hands whapped the table-top. "They need to talk to me. I need to know. I realize Phyllis is sick. I know she has cancer, multiple myeloma. But what does that mean?"

I felt focused as the kitchen melted away into my peripheral vision, leaving only a concerned and confused mother spotlighted before me. My words emerged from an unknown inner place as if the wisdom I had gained from my own pain—not knowing details about my sister's illness—was speaking for me. "Well, she'll have treatment, like chemotherapy . . ."

"And then what?" Violet snapped.

"Well, um, hopefully the chemotherapy will relieve some of the symptoms." I paused and shifted in my seat again. "But, well, at this point there's no cure for Phyllis's type of cancer." I paused again. "It's incurable."

Violet rubbed her hands together so vigorously that her purse knocked against the table. "So . . . so, is Phyllis going to die?"

I could hear myself swallow. "Yes. There's no cure," I said, avoiding her eyes.

Quietly, Violet replied, "Thank you."

And then, very loudly, she wailed, "Why? Why her? Why not me? I'm eighty years old, for chrissake. I've lived my life. Phyllis is young, a child . . ."

She stood up, screeching her chair across the linoleum so loudly that I couldn't hear the rest of her sentence. The front door opened and thumped shut.

A moment later, Phyllis appeared in the kitchen doorway wearing a jewel-purple shirt, crimson lipstick, and too much blush.

"Where's Mom?" she asked.

"She left." That was all I said. I didn't mention the conversation to Phyllis or anyone else.

Phyllis flapped a piece of notebook paper at me. "Here's the list."

With that, although I didn't know it then, she introduced me to the routine of subsequent visits. Errands—Albertson's, Post Office, Credit Union—and the day's agenda, which could include stops at the art store or Goodwill. I'd drive; Phyllis would direct. Just the two of us. Marc stayed at the house in Apalachicola.

That first Friday evening we sat on her bed folding laundry, both wearing thermal shirts and glasses. I thought we looked alike.

We hugged goodnight and I moved to the den with the "pull-out" across the hall. Our doors remained open a crack. I heard pill bottles opening, Phyllis coughing, and then quiet. I stared at the low ceiling draped in shadow and savored the difference between this and my loft bedroom. No traffic or emergency vehicles here, only the tiptoeing of cats and the songs of cicadas crooning to their sweethearts.

On Sunday, it was already time for me to leave so I'd be ready for my Atlanta workweek. Phyllis and I had developed a plan for when we weren't together: a once-a-week phone call, every Wednesday at 2:00 p.m.

I glanced out the car window as I pulled out of the driveway to find Phyllis standing in the yard grinning and flashing a peace sign. I kept her in view, checking my mirror, as I drove up the street and out of her neighborhood, making my way to I-75 N.

58

I entered our phone date in my work calendar as "meeting" and assigned it as "recurring."

Each Wednesday afternoon, I'd gather a soft-sided, spiral-bound note-book, a cup of tea or coffee, and await Phyllis's call. We typically spoke for an hour, the amount of time it took for her portable phone to crackle or for fatigue to diminish her voice to a whisper. I took copious notes, capturing Phyllis's exact words as a way, I later realized, to settle myself. And today, I still have them all these years later. Phyllis's words—their humor and angst—remain on those pages.

Phyllis called promptly at 2:00 p.m.

After a quick greeting, she'd launch into her stories as if an audio engineer had signaled to her. A recurring series—which would certainly be a podcast today—was *All About Hair*, her iconic long dark hair that, over the years, she had trimmed herself by pulling a handful from the back and cutting the ends.

"I've lost an appendage," she said, now that she had cropped her hair short. "I never realized how much I used my hair. I twisted and flipped it, and I wadded it up on my neck when I needed a pillow. I'm always cold now. When I comb it, only a few hairs fall out. I was told that before it really comes out, your scalp gets sensitive. My head is starting to feel sore, so maybe it's going to happen soon."

The following Wednesday, the hair stories continued. "I went out for the first time since my haircut, and to a concert, no less. I wore that red tam I have—you know; the one with the sequins on it—and big, sparkly earrings with dangling feathers. I felt conspicuous, like everyone was looking at me, and Marc said, 'They are. You're stunning.' At intermission, I went to the la-dies' room and there were so many women with beautiful hair. I couldn't stop looking at them. I wasn't envious; I was just in love with their hair."

I could hear Phyllis taking a long sip from the straw in her water bottle, then she continued as if she were doing stand-up with one story leading into another. "It started on Sunday. My scalp felt like it was sunburned, so sensitive, and you won't believe this, I actually got a stiff neck from trying to suck it in. I wanted to hold on to the hair I had left. Can you imagine? A stiff neck. From sucking in my scalp. Really bad, like whiplash.

"Yesterday in the shower, it happened. My hair just started coming out. Wads of it. Took me hours to clean up the bathroom, and I still don't think I got it all. I couldn't blow dry my hair; it would fly all over the place. So weird. I still have my bangs. They just keep hangin' on."

When our calls ended, I'd sit and stare and breathe, noticing my exhale. In and out. I'd study sun streaks emerging from my large windows and watch the light diffuse into a late afternoon stillness. Serenity had made its home in my downtown loft. I tried to stay in that peace and push aside the fact that one day, we would no longer have a weekly call.

I fixated on the mantra that would end up guiding me for the remainder of this journey. *Be present. Enjoy the time you have left. Laugh together. Support Phyllis in the way she wants to live (and die).*

The ring of the phone rattled me out of my reverie. Phyllis had forgotten to tell me about a "Laying on of Hands," a healing ceremony that would take place in two weeks.

I arrived in Tallahassee the evening before the gathering.

On the day of the ceremony, the Dancing Girls arrived over the course of the morning, each fawning over Phyllis with questions about her health. Annie, a palm reader, touted the power of crystals, especially clear quartz. Joan shared her research on clinical trials, and Carole repeatedly suggested Phyllis sit down. *Let us get you this...and that...and...* Congenial chaos reigned with everyone talking at once. Phyllis grabbed my arm and pulled me aside into the small hallway by the bathroom.

"I don't like this. All they talk about is sickness. It makes me feel sick." Her shoulders caved; her arms hung limp against her sides.

I nodded. I understood. From that point on, I would be Phyllis's front-person, the one to filter comments. Back with the group, I stood guard between Phyllis and the Dancing Girls as we waited for the Deacon.

Before long, we spied him walking up the path. He looked distinguished and wise in his black clergy attire. When he saw us peering out the window, he smiled.

Throughout the next half-hour, the house pulsated with animated conversation and raucous laughter until the Deacon requested our presence on the deck. Our voices lowered to whispers, perhaps because he called it "a healing ceremony."

The sliding glass door opened with effort and a gravelly sound. One by one, we filed out, positioning our chairs in a circle. Someone dragged out a stool for Phyllis. Apparently, she and the Deacon had already discussed "Laying on of Hands" and she didn't want to lie down; instead, she would sit above us.

I placed my chair slightly outside the circle and sat facing the backyard. The houses on all sides disappeared behind bamboo and towering Florida pines. In front of me, an expanse of often-not-mowed grass suggested a meadow, and around us, bird feeders, wind chimes, and a plastic rainbow hung from low tree branches. At my side, a sapling emerged from a hole in the deck's planks, creating an umbrella of shade and a playground for squirrels.

At the Deacon's instruction, the Dancing Girls placed their hands on Phyllis's arms. The Deacon rested his hands on her shoulders. I reached into the web of limbs and placed my hand on her knee, slightly turning my back to the group. I needed my own space. I tilted my head upward, closed my eyes, and felt the sun's warmth. The air was still, as if holding its breath.

The Deacon began: "Oh, most merciful God, God of love and mercy, whose desire is always to heal. God who knows our needs before we ask, who wants only good for us, God, three in one, Holy Spirit, work through our hands to heal our dear friend Phyllis . . ." And in a tone meant for us, he said, "Join me with your prayers . . ."

Soon, our murmurs—Christian, Jewish, and New Age—merged together into one bidding of hope. I took long, deep breaths. As my chest filled, I imagined pulling all the dark, gross disease from Phyllis's body. As I slowly exhaled, I envisioned glowing pink light moving from me and encircling her.

After a while, a Towhee bird sang a closing hymn. *Whooo-eet. Whooo-eet.*

When I returned to Atlanta, neighbors and vagrants alike greeted me as I made my way from the parking deck to my loft with my overloaded tote bags—projects left undone. I felt cheered by the welcome, but once settled, the dissonant sounds of traffic grated on my nerves. I collapsed onto my bed without undressing and slept for ten hours.

Our Wednesday phone calls continued with a comforting familiarity. My online calendar would alert me, I'd prepare tea, grab a notebook, and wait for Phyllis's call, which was never more than a few minutes off our two o'clock agreement. Her "hello" always included her whispery laugh, so that I often didn't catch all of her words. She'd ask about my week, a recounting that I kept short, and then she'd launch into her stories. We'd laugh our way through them.

The hair series continued.

"I wake up at all times of the night. The other night I awoke with cartoons on my mind. Ideas for a cartoon strip, 'Cancer Comics.' Do you think that's too morbid? I was thinking about calling the newspaper to see if I could do a series. So, here's my first one. It's a takeoff on the Tina Turner song, 'What's Love Got to Do with It,' but it's 'What's Hair Got to Do with It.' Imagine Cher without hair. Goldie Hawn. Then there's me without hair. We've all had the same hairdo for thirty years.

"I picked up a wig at the cancer society. It's poufy, like a 1950s housewife. It's still in the box. I think I'd like a Cleopatra wig instead."

As the weeks went by, she'd relate her struggles with being sick more often. "They're giving me melphalan, and I take Kytril for nausea, steroids for energy, and Valium to make sure I don't have too much energy. This gets ridiculous."

"Oh my," I interjected. I didn't take any medicine; I couldn't imagine keeping track of all that.

"I had a high temperature, 102 degrees," Phyllis continued. "The doctor said I was in my low resistance week, so he called in an antibiotic. There I was, lying in the bed with an ice pack on my forehead because I was burning up, and at the same time, a heater right next to me because I was shivering.

"Vince and Marc were sitting at the foot of my bed going back and forth about who was going to pick up my prescriptions. 'You go.' 'No, you go.' 'You've been driving all day; I'll go.' 'No, you go and take my car; it's more comfortable.' This went on and on until I said, 'I'll go and I'll walk there.' So, that did it. They both went. What a circus. I'll take one woman for ten men any day."

After we'd hung up, I'd always sit for a while before returning to my desk to work. I'd breathe deliberately—a quick meditation of sorts—and watch the light patterns grace the wood floor. Then, I'd close my notebook, clean up my tea service, and return to my latest contract assignment.

Photos of Phyllis and the Dancing Girls were taped around my computer monitor. The feathers that Phyllis had secretly tucked into my tote bags emerged from a jar like a bouquet. I never knew what to expect when I unpacked. During the last trip, Phyllis had slipped a small grocery bag tied with a ribbon into my suitcase. Across it, she had drawn a heart with a Sharpie inscribed with the words, *Thank you, Fil-us.* Inside was a child's box of raisins, red-wrapped chocolate hearts, and a bright turquoise feather.

CHAPTER 12

Tampa Road Trip

SEVEN MONTHS AFTER Phyllis's diagnosis, she called, and it wasn't a Wednesday. The indignation and disgust in her voice startled me.

"Go to your house near the beach and paint," she said. "Can you believe that? That's what he told me."

I wasn't clear if these were the Tallahassee oncologist's words or Phyllis's interpretation of them, but her response was precise and expected.

"I'm getting another opinion."

She had already been to the Mayo Clinic and the Shand's Cancer Hospital but wasn't content with what those doctors had told her either. So we agreed I would accompany her to the Moffitt Cancer Center in Tampa. Our starting point: Apalachicola, "our" house near the beach.

I crossed the bridge and wound my way into town on a late afternoon in July, my birthday. The digital sign outside the bank read 104 degrees. The heat had rendered everything still, no one was walking or driving or pulling in fishing nets.

"Happy Birthday," Phyllis shouted as she swung open the creaky screen door to greet me. "I've baked cupcakes. We can drive over the bridge to St.

George's Island to celebrate."

Phyllis appeared oblivious to the triple-digit temperature as she whirled around the house preparing for our picnic and road trip. She wore cruise-wear from the 1940s: a halter dress, layers of beaded necklaces, feathered earrings, and a blue polka-dotted bandana over her chemo-bald head. Quite a contrast to my khaki shorts, t-shirt, and sturdy sneakers. The heat had swollen my fingers, and freckles continued to sprout across my face.

Before we left, Phyllis snapped a birthday photo with my new Polaroid Joycam, a present to myself. The three-by-two-inch image popped out like magic: me next to the door with the porch light over my head, and another mysterious glow inside the house.

Phyllis peered over my shoulder and hummed. "My spirit angels. Look, two shining lights. You and Hilda."

Ah, so Hilda, the ghost, was still around.

As if reading my thoughts, Phyllis added, "I find drawers open after I know I've closed them, and I hear tapping in my closet. I believe Hilda's happy I live here, but she wants to make sure I know it's still her house. She's stubborn like that."

Isn't stubbornness or tenacity one of Phyllis's traits? Maybe there was something to this relationship with Hilda.

Once at the beach, I held the Joycam at arm's length to capture a portrait of the two of us, ending up with just the tops of our heads, Phyllis in her blue bandana and me in mine, a feeble show of solidarity. True solidarity would be shaving my head, which my vanity would never allow. I relied on my long, wavy, red hair for confidence and second glances from strangers, a most delightful experience.

The sand, the Gulf, and the evening sky belonged to us along with a few seagulls arguing over their potential dinner of cupcake crumbs. We sang "Happy Birthday," conducting an imaginary orchestra that shooed away the birds, then scarfed down our tiny cakes, laughing and taking more photos. Afterward, we dragged our beach towels to the water's edge and sat in silence. A slight breeze billowed the water into low rolling waves that kissed our toes and then swirled around our ankles.

After a while, with her gaze set on the horizon, Phyllis spoke in a raspy whisper. "My father visited me in a dream. Twice."

She turned her face to mine. "I told him I was sick, and he said he already knew. Now I feel his presence all the time and I regularly talk to him."

The setting sun bathed her in dramatic cadmium yellow light that reminded me of photographs I had seen of the Italian coast. "Cadmium," I said to myself, a word that artists know from paint tubes and watercolor blocks. Phyllis and her father, Maxi, both artists. Forever connected. I marveled at our soul's expansive existence.

Early the next morning we headed out like hippies traveling to Woodstock. Phyllis surprised me by getting behind the wheel. "You've already done a lot of driving just to get here."

The van only had a bench seat in front. In the back, tote bags of clothes, shoeboxes of cassette tapes, bookbags, and snacks were packed like a Rubik's cube. No one seeing us would have imagined we were driving five hours to a cancer center for a fourth opinion.

I placed my feet on the dashboard and turned down the brim of my ballcap against the morning sun, which was already scorching the treetops. We slipped by hushed houses with their inhabitants either still asleep or immobile because at 7:00 a.m. the bank sign already displayed 98 degrees.

By mid-Florida, the landscape opened up to the expanse I loved: wide flat stretches of green and a half-globe of brilliant blue with astonishing and always-changing clouds. Phyllis and I chatted, sang along to Carol King, and stopped at roadside stands for souvenirs.

On the outskirts of Tampa, we took a break for lunch and gas. Because the van didn't have a gas gauge, Phyllis had to calculate gas stops according to mileage and an estimated distance per gallon. We spotted a sandwich shop nearby in a deserted strip mall. Phyllis, the vegetarian, wanted a smoothie; I requested a chicken sandwich. We sat inside along the wall at a small, chipped Formica-topped table.

When we returned to the van, Phyllis climbed into the passenger side. "You're better at city driving."

We arrived at the Moffitt Cancer Center in plenty of time for Phyllis's afternoon appointment. The lobby reminded me of the posh Florida hotels where I used to attend statewide art education conferences. Gigantic plants, abstract paintings, a skylight saturated with sunlight. I looked around trying to grasp that I was really in a hospital as Phyllis disappeared into a restroom.

She returned wearing make-up, a sundress instead of her shorts, and her poufy wig, while I was still grubby in my t-shirt and tennis shoes.

"You look like you're going to a party," I said.

"Well," she chuckled, "I guess I am."

I smiled. Feeling like a chaperone for a teen dance, I led her through the lobby, the elevators, and another lobby. While we waited, Phyllis squirmed, giggled, and uttered sentences so filled with her humming laughter that I couldn't follow her discourse. I, on the other hand, remained on high alert. Nuance in the receptionist's voice— what did she mean by "good luck to you"? No eye contact from hospital staff crisscrossing our path. Why weren't they acknowledging us?

We were soon ushered into a room that felt like a classroom, institutional with cinderblock walls painted celery-green and windows along one side. Phyllis and I sat in plastic chairs with metal legs facing the front where I visualized a chalkboard. My ever-present notebook was lying across my thighs.

A young man wearing dark blue scrubs, with close-cropped hair and a pleasant smile, introduced himself as a physician's assistant.

"We reviewed your records," he said, opening a folder, "and, of course, if you decide to be treated here, we will do extensive testing. As you may know, your particular cancer is staged from one to three, like other types of cancers that you may be familiar with. Stage 1 means no noticeable symptoms and Stage 3 is the most advanced. In the case of multiple myeloma, Stage 3 means the red blood cells have dropped to a low level, anemia is severe, calcium in the bloodstream has greatly risen, and three or more bones are affected. We agree with your Tallahassee oncologist that you are in Stage 2, but we disagree with the severity."

Phyllis audibly sucked in her breath, and I sat upright so my back no longer curved into the bend of the plastic chair.

The physician's assistant continued. "Within each stage are further delineations depending on kidney function, so the cancer may be in Stage 2A or Stage 2B and so on. We believe that you are in a lesser delineation of Stage 2 than you were originally told by the doctors in Tallahassee."

Phyllis and I turned to each other and smiled. As I opened my mouth to whisper *good news,* the door crashed open. A man and a woman wearing white jackets stepped into the room. The woman carried a clipboard.

Phyllis shifted in her seat, smiled, and opened the folder on her lap. I glanced over, wondering why I hadn't noticed the folder before now. The stack of papers inside was topped with a Sunday magazine clipping featuring a picture of the man who had just entered and a bold heading that I couldn't quite read. I got the gist; he was a prominent cancer researcher. Phyllis had circled the article with a thick marker and drawn hearts and a star over the doctor's head.

Why hadn't she mentioned this to me? I finally connected the dots. This doctor was her savior, her rock star. This explained the change of clothing and the wig.

As he introduced himself and his nurse, Phyllis clutched the folder to her chest, looked up at him, and beamed. From then on, I called him "The Renowned Researcher."

He sidestepped to center position in front of my imagined chalkboard; the others moved aside. His hair was dark and swept back, his voice smooth. A thick air of confidence surrounded him, confirming his celebrity status. He gazed at Phyllis and me and an illusory audience behind us—a full lecture hall—and restated the obvious. "Multiple myeloma is incurable . . ."

Now he was in his element explaining his team's research with stem cell transplants. He eventually paused, and with a thunderous, "Therefore," laid out his proposal for Phyllis. "Maintenance is our goal. A stem cell transplant could get you to a plateau, and we would maintain the cancer at that level for as long as possible. It's like managing diabetes. There is no cure for diabetes, but people live many years because it's managed. The longer you live, the more likelihood you have of getting into a clinical trial for one of the new cancer drugs."

I glanced at Phyllis who appeared transfixed, her mouth slightly parted as if songs of joy were poised to tumble out.

As the Renowned Researcher flung out his arm, his nurse handed him the clipboard, and he moved toward us. On a blank sheet of paper, he drew a diagram that looked like a mountain range. "Here are the stages of your cancer . . ." and pointing to a plateau, ". . . here is the ideal time for maintenance. This is our goal with a stem cell transplant."

He continued talking, but I blanked out for a minute. This seemed too good to be true, too easy. Why hadn't anyone mentioned this before? This was Phyllis's *fourth* opinion, for goodness' sake.

The Renowned Researcher went on to say Phyllis had three options. I scrawled the number "3" on a notebook page.

"You could have your standard chemotherapy along with pain management drugs," he said, citing the Tallahassee oncologist's recommendation. "Or you could decide on thalidomide, a drug that blocks blood vessel growth . . ."

What? I remembered the *Life* magazine images of babies missing arms or toes or fingers because their mothers had been given thalidomide for morning sickness. Was thalidomide now being used to halt the spread of cancerous cells?

The Renowned Researcher backed up, handed the clipboard to the nurse without looking at her, and paused. After a few seconds, he slowly raised his eyes and focused them directly on Phyllis. "Or you could select high-dose chemotherapy with a stem cell transplant."

He explained the procedure. Low-dose chemo destroys cancer and normal cells. High-dose chemo does that too, but a stem cell transplant replenishes the bone marrow with new normal cells.

I wondered how much Phyllis was grasping.

I tried to memorize the key facts. First, normal stem cells are extracted from the patient and then stored and frozen. After high-dose chemo kills the patient's cancer cells, the stored normal cells are defrosted and infused. It takes four weeks for them to find their way through the bloodstream to the bone marrow and to start producing new cancer-free cells. A hospital stay is required because the patient must be closely monitored.

Years later I would describe the procedure this way: "Basically, they kill you and then they bring you back to life."

The Renowned Researcher held out his hands, palms up, as if offering Phyllis a gift. "High-dose chemotherapy with a stem cell transplant has been very successful for many patients, especially those like you who are in their fifties and have adequate kidney and heart function. Some of these patients remain in the maintenance stage for many years. This is my recommendation."

With that, and "We'll give you a minute," they left the room. I turned to Phyllis, making sure her gaze was directly on mine. I wanted her full attention as I recapped my understanding of the meeting.

"You have three options . . ." I began. I listed and explained them all, my voice even, neutral, and not showing preference.

Before Phyllis could respond, the door opened, and the research team marched in again. The Renowned Researcher looked directly at Phyllis awaiting her decision, but she was mute. When I spoke instead, his head ticked toward me. I detected annoyance in his eyes.

"Phyllis could continue with standard chemotherapy, or she could select thalidomide," I said.

He nodded.

"If the thalidomide treatment didn't work, Phyllis could still have a stem cell transplant."

He nodded again and let out a sigh that was more like a low growl.

"Both thalidomide and a stem cell transplant could bring Phyllis to the desired maintenance plateau, correct?" I asked.

He pursed his lips. "Yes."

I pressed on. "The thalidomide treatment is much less of an ordeal and less invasive that the stem cell transplant."

"Yes." He nodded, rocked back and forth on his heels, and clasped his hands behind his back.

"Has anyone died from the thalidomide treatment?"

He shook his head.

"What about the stem cell transplant? Has anyone died from the procedure and not from the cancer?"

"Yes, but a very low percentage."

That was all I needed. I knew the option I would select, but the words came from Phyllis. "I want the thalidomide treatment," she said with strong conviction in her voice.

We wriggled in our plastic chairs and our legs touched. We smiled.

"That's exactly what I would have said," I told her. "My words came out of your mouth, or I guess it was really your words and my thoughts, well, your thoughts too, of course . . . Hey! Where did everyone go?"

We waited. Surely, they would return to comment on Phyllis's decision and say goodbye. Several minutes passed before the door opened and another man in dark blue scrubs, whom we hadn't met, walked in.

"I'm here to give you training," he said.

Phyllis and I looked at each other, turned toward the assistant, then back at each other.

"Oh," he said, deciphering our questioning looks. "They only deal with stem cell transplants. You've chosen thalidomide so I'm here. The government requires that anyone coming into contact with thalidomide has training. Here's a list of dos and don'ts. Please read them and then indicate by your signatures that you understand the implications."

He handed us each a single sheet—the training—which we both read and signed.

"Moffitt will contact you to set up appointments," he added. "You'll need a check-up about every four weeks."

Then he thanked us and directed us to the pharmacy for the thalidomide. "After you pick up the meds, you're free to leave."

Easy.

Three months later in October, Phyllis called me. "The thalidomide is working. There are some side effects—numbness in my feet, sometimes my hands tingle, and I'm often tired—but I can live with them. "Oh, one more thing. I have hair!"

That December, the Dancing Girls gathered for our annual holiday dinner to exchange homemade presents and mug for the camera like we always did. But who selected a Mexican restaurant? Couldn't our gathering be hosted at someone's home, as in the past? I pictured candles and evergreens, rather than glaring overhead lights and maracas. The setting—odd and misplaced— seemed to match our mood. We sat at a long rectangle table, so it was hard to talk to anyone not sitting nearby. Perhaps nobody knew what to say. I had a sad premonition that it might be our last Christmas together.

The New Year rolled in unceremoniously and in May of 2001, a year and five months since Phyllis's diagnosis, Marc developed a listserv of friends and family so he could easily send updates about Phyllis's condition.

From our phone calls, I knew she was no longer responding to thalidomide, but on a subsequent Wednesday call, hope reverberated in her words. "Moffitt told me I'm a good candidate for a clinical trial."

So it seemed we had selected the best option, after all.

Marc's email a week later changed everything.

Email [from Marc listserv]

Sent: Tues, 29 May 2001 11:49

They discovered something wrong with Phyllis's kidneys, so she was admitted to the hospital where she is getting a saline solution infusion.

When we were in Tampa on the 11th, the doctor took her off thalidomide because it wasn't working. She was scheduled to start the clinical trial drug FTI. The doctor said that this is the brightest time in multiple myeloma research because they are now finding target-based drugs (attacking the myeloma cells at the molecular level). Unfortunately, Phyllis had to undergo a painful procedure and chose to take morphine for the pain, and she had a terrible reaction to it.

Now her kidneys have to be back to normal before she can participate in a trial.

Damn. I shut down my computer and stared at the blank screen. Damn. What next?

CHAPTER 13

Decisions

NON-RESPONSIVE TO thalidomide, compromised kidney functioning, participation in clinical trial denied. What now? The Renowned Researcher said Phyllis was still eligible for a stem cell transplant, but did she really want one?

The two of us announced a resurrection of the "Anniversary Party" to bring the girlfriends together to help her sort through the options. We'd make a collective decision about her next steps.

Ignoring the severe weather forecast, the Dancing Girls gathered at a house on Alligator Point, an hour south of Tallahassee. We expected a weekend-long slumber party. Hopefully, we could help Phyllis and also be silly again much like our parties in the past.

For eight years after Kiki's marriage had fallen apart, we had gathered on August 3rd, Kiki's wedding anniversary, to recreate the original party with all its craziness and precious female bonding. Phyllis would remind us of the date and shepherd us to Kiki's pool. But over time, our lives had established new loyalties: both Kiki and Annie remarried, Joan discovered true love, and Carole and I had moved away from Tallahassee. The "Anniversary Party" evolved from a recurring event to a hilarious story.

But now, Phyllis's decision was crucial, an emergency. Certainly we'd reunite for Phyllis and call it an "Anniversary Party" no matter the date, year, or place.

The house we had borrowed for the weekend sat proudly on stilts surrounded by pines and untamed shrubs. It must have been a summer home to now grown children who once fished off the dock, gathered fireflies in jars, and played gin rummy for pennies. Joan's friend said we could use it. No one would be there that weekend, so come get the key.

The front door opened into that family's past, but the back door faced St. George's Sound and unlocked possibilities for us to make our own memories. The sky appeared vast, and the bulbous clouds had yet to become threatening. I breathed in a wet freshness like laundry on a line and hoped it was a good omen. I would facilitate the decision-making, something I did skillfully with clients. When we left, Phyllis would know what to do; *yes* or *no* to a stem cell transplant.

Wary of the impending storm, we retreated to an area off the kitchen for the big discussion rather than sitting out back. Phyllis, Annie, and I sat in a row on a rattan couch as if in a waiting room. Carole had plunked herself into a deep-cushioned club chair, Joan stood, and Kiki paced.

For what seemed like hours no one spoke, which allowed me to size up the room: dark paneled walls, tattered rugs piled on top of a linoleum floor, a small lamp giving off a yellow-tinged glow. An old radio crooned jazz without much static considering the storm brewing to the west.

"You'll need resources," Joan finally said, facing us like a presenter leading a break-out group. "My co-worker's father had a stem cell transplant and good god, they were organized. It's necessary. You'll need meals prepared, and someone to clean-up because everything must be kept completely sanitary."

"And Jimmy," interrupted Carole. "He'll need to skip at least one semester, come home, and help out."

Phyllis's torso shot forward, and her voice stuttered as if she had more thoughts than words. "No, I'm not involving my son. He can call, we can talk.

But it took me years to get him to go to college. I'm not taking the chance that he won't finish school. I want him to stay where he is."

We all nodded. Once Phyllis had made up her mind, especially when it came to Jimmy, there was no changing it.

Joan cleared her throat and continued to relate her co-worker's experience as if she had notecards. "Their pets went to friends' houses for several months. The family missed them, but it was necessary because of the dander. I'm not sure you'd be able to keep Spotless and the cats while you're recovering."

I felt Phyllis squirm as if she were about to speak, but then Kiki chimed in, her hands on her hips. "Phyllis, you take care of everyone. If you had a stem cell transplant, you would need to have people take care of you."

In the silence that followed, I noticed the musty air from our closed-in space and wondered if we all had the same thought: Marc. Marc with a c. Marc, Phyllis's live-in boyfriend who had asked her to marry him and to whom she replied, "I've been married twice. That's enough." Marc, the talented musician, who sang Ragtime for the crowd and cried the blues to Phyllis. That Marc. He would have to step up.

In a voice I hadn't heard from her before, one that pronounced every vowel and consonant, Phyllis said, "Marc takes care of me. He's the one who massages my feet in the middle of the night when they go numb. He's the one who holds my head and pats my back when I'm vomiting. I gave him a chance to pull out. I told him that he didn't sign up for this. And you see what his response was, don't you? He stayed."

None of us replied; instead, we avoided each other's eyes until the lights flickered and the radio crackled.

"Storm's coming," said Kiki. We all agreed, and I realized my failure as a facilitator. Nothing had been decided.

Carole eased herself out of the club chair and ambled to the kitchen. Before long, we were bumping shoulders as we prepared sandwiches and opened bottles of beer. We laughed about past Anniversary Parties—recounting the first one like we always did—and gossiped.

The stem cell transplant conversation disappeared into the shadows.

At dawn, while the tropical storm mustered its forces into hurricane status, we decided to leave. Rain pelted us as we rushed up and down the stairs of the house wearing bathing suits and wrapped in beach towels, the best we could do for protective gear. Phyllis waited in my car.

Once packed, I joined her, our visibility almost zero as if we were sitting in a carwash. We'd wait until everyone was ready to go and the house was locked before we'd all leave in a caravan.

"Let's put on lipstick," I shouted over the pounding rain.

"Yes," screamed Phyllis.

Simultaneously, we flipped down the overhead car mirrors and soon turned to each other— very pink-mouthed—and laughed, the sound obscured by the storm.

"Remember that movie?" Phyllis said. "Remember the line, 'Don't let me die without my eyebrows'?"

"Yes, yes," I responded.

Phyllis's smile vanished as she looked directly at me, but her eyes twinkled as she assumed Shirley MacLaine's role for herself. "Don't let me die without eyeliner, lipstick, and a little mascara," she said.

I nodded as my chest tightened. This was the first time I heard Phyllis acknowledge her death.

Once back at her house, she and I huddled in the dining area—the table barely showing beneath piles of papers—while the rain assaulted the windowpanes with enough force to mute Marc's piano playing in the next room.

Feeling safe and dry, we pulled that nagging decision about a stem cell transplant back into the light.

Phyllis handed me an inch-thick packet from the Moffitt Cancer Center. Her expression said, *you know I will never read something like this, please take a look, and help me figure it out.*

"Can you make sense of this?" she asked aloud, placing the bulging packet in my hands.

I pulled out charts from the folder's pockets; Phyllis brewed tea.

After scanning the material, I said, "Let's compare.

"Under 'Benefits,' there are two items: Contributing to medical research . . ." to which we responded in unison, "Screw that."

". . . and your life may be, but not guaranteed to be, prolonged for a period of time."

"As for 'Risks' . . ."

I held up several pages—small print, single-spaced—and waved them at Phyllis. I read them aloud, skimming over the hard-to-read medical jargon, and added, "Check this out. You could have diarrhea and you could be constipated, so I guess, they cancel each other out and you'll be fine."

I placed the papers on the table and turned to Phyllis, waiting until she looked directly at me before I spoke.

"Here are the possibilities. One, you could have a stem cell transplant. They would freeze your good cells, give you high-dose chemo to kill the cancerous cells, and then put your good cells back so they could produce new cancer-free cells. Sounds simple, but it's a horrific procedure. High-dose chemotherapy is very powerful. But you could live for a number of years. In that time, they could find a cure for your cancer. If not, you will die."

Phyllis blinked and nodded for me to continue. "Or, two, you could have a stem cell transplant, that same horrific procedure, and live for only a short amount of time—there's no guarantee how well it will work—and if a cure for your cancer isn't found, you will die."

She rocked forward a bit, awaiting what she may have known was coming next.

"Or, three, you could have low-dose chemotherapy without the horrific procedure, something that's familiar, live for a short period of time and if a cure for your cancer isn't found, you will die."

I believed she got the picture, and I knew explicitly what I would choose for myself. I would have gone to the house near the beach and paint, just as her Tallahassee oncologist had told her ten months prior. I had long ago made peace with death, which didn't scare me as much as pain from complicated medical procedures. Easy decision for me; I wasn't the one with the terminal diagnosis. I had to put my feelings aside and stay true to the mantra: *support Phyllis in the way she wants to live and die.*

Phyllis must have made a decision. She grinned and sat very upright in the dining chair. "I'm not going to do it," she said. "I'm not going to have a stem cell transplant. It's too much for me to go through and the outcome is the same. I choose number three. I want low-dose chemo, and I'd like for you to write a letter to the Moffitt Cancer Center with my decision. Also, please add that I'm interested in a clinical trial when one becomes available."

"Okay, then. It's decided."

We beamed, pleased with our progress, just as Marc burst into the living room like a bouncing puppy missing out on the fun.

"I heard you laughing even through all the rain and thunder. What's going on?"

"I've made a decision," Phyllis replied. "I'm not going to have a stem cell transplant. I'm going to have low-dose chemo."

Her statement halted Marc in his path, and he let out an agonizing groan. "What? What? What are you talking about? What are you thinking?" He threw back his head and beseeched the heavens with upraised arms.

Phyllis stood up, appearing taller than usual. "I'm sticking with low-dose chemo."

Marc moved toward her, ignoring me as if I were off-stage in this discussion. "Why did you even go to Alligator Point? I thought your girlfriends were going to convince you to have a stem cell transplant."

I stared at Phyllis and then at Marc. Was *that* the plan?

Marc paced back and forth waving his arms, shouting. "There are testimonials out there. Real stories, real people with multiple myeloma, who have lived for five years after the transplant. Five years! In five years, there'll be new drugs and clinical trials. After five years, you could have another transplant. That's ten years. None of us are guaranteed ten years. A stem cell transplant is the only way to go."

Phyllis remained stoic, legs firmly planted, and silent.

I stood and stepped between the two of them, facing Marc. "It was never the girlfriends' intention to convince Phyllis of anything. She has to make this decision for herself. We'll support her in any decision she makes."

Marc backed up a bit and grumbled to himself.

I repeated myself. "We don't want to convince Phyllis. We want her to make her own decision."

Marc groaned. "You don't know what you're talking about," he said without looking at me or Phyllis. He threw up his arms again in a gesture that said *you're crazy* and stomped back to the den and his piano.

Phyllis and I looked at each other. The storm inside the house had ended, but the one outside continued to rage.

She was the first to speak. "When you write that letter to Moffitt would you add, 'Can my boyfriend have the transplant for me?'" she said with a smirk.

CHAPTER 14

Tampa Again

A MONTH LATER, Phyllis called on a Tuesday. "Would you take the first week?"

I didn't understand the chagrin I heard in Phyllis's voice or what she was talking about.

"Vince will take the second week, and Marc the third."

"What?" I got up from my work area and paced over to the couch. A long pause dangled between us.

Phyllis eventually broke the silence. "I'm going to have a stem cell transplant. I need family members—and you're my sister, remember—to stay with me while I'm in the hospital for three weeks."

I repositioned the handset tucked into the crook of my neck. After all we've been through, she was going to go ahead and have it? What in the world had changed her mind?

Phyllis continued, "Marc and I went to Moffitt, and I told them, just as you and I discussed, that I wanted low-dose chemo. I was firm and I spoke up. You would have been proud. They said fine, they would transfer my care to Tallahassee. 'Tallahassee?' I said, and that's when they explained that the research group at Moffitt only does stem cell transplants. Low-dose chemo would be administered by my Tallahassee oncologist."

She paused, and I tried to picture the conversation. Imagining Phyllis's split-second change of heart was easy. Of course, the Renowned Researcher.

"I couldn't leave him," she said.

I understood. Phyllis loved her rock star and was repelled by the Tallahassee oncologist whom she called "Dr. Gloom and Doom."

In October 2001, almost two years after her diagnosis, I met Phyllis at her Tallahassee home for our second road trip, four hours to Tampa. The plan was for me to drive. So on a mild and Florida-sunny morning, I stood by her van while she paraded one tote bag after another and loaded each into the back.

"I have to do this myself," she said.

A large tote bag marked with orange ribbons held her clothes in sealed plastic bags. That would go to the hospital. Several blue-ribboned tote bags contained supplies to stock the apartment across the street where I, and then Vince, and then Marc would stay, and where she would transition after the procedure. A tropical patterned flamingo tote bag bulged with our art projects.

I climbed into the driver's seat and watched Phyllis close up the house. Before long, she joined me with an easy-breezy smile. On her wrist was the beaded bracelet that matched mine, and hanging around her neck was a St. Christopher medal and a silk patterned pouch—purple, pink, and blue—the size of a half-dollar. Phyllis tugged the drawstring open to reveal the quartz crystal I had given her at Annie's recommendation—Divine Power—and a tiny plastic bag.

"Sand from Saint George's Island," she hummed.

I smiled and paused before backing out of her driveway. For a brief moment, the space between Phyllis and me was pregnant with tranquility. The gods were aligned. I felt confident and grounded, and I knew my purpose: move forward in faith.

We stopped at gas stations several times for Phyllis to stretch her swollen legs. I cringed watching her grimace as she circled a patch of pavement by the van. She labored with each step; her brow furrowed. But, back in the passenger seat, she relaxed, leaning her head back and smiling peacefully.

"It's the anti-anxiety medication," she whispered without me asking.

Everything amped up as we approached the exit for Moffitt. Phyllis opened the thick manilla folder on her lap and flitted through all the papers, fidgeted with the straw of her ever-present water bottle, and periodically emitted a nervous laugh.

As we pulled into the parking lot, I turned to her and asked, "How are you?"

"Terrified."

The hospital lobby presented a labyrinth of doors, elevators, and hallways, and no longer appeared posh to me. Phyllis's eyes darted everywhere like a wary terrier going to the vet.

"Where's the research team? I don't see anyone I know," she said.

"It'll work out," I replied as I took her hand and led her to check-in.

Within ten minutes, a nurse practitioner whisked Phyllis away for admittance tests. I released a long sigh. She was okay now. The process was in motion. No more empty time for thinking.

Phyllis's first room had an antechamber leading to a larger vaulted space. She reclined on the bed with her back against the wall, clutching the folder of papers and her water bottle, while I sat in the straight-back chair next to her holding a steno pad like a secretary. I had decided this journal would stay with whomever was caring for Phyllis. When I left, it would be relayed to Vince, who would pass it on to Marc. I wondered if the guys would really bother taking notes and what the pages would reveal a month from now. For now, the pages were empty.

Phyllis and I sat together and stared at the open door with the harsh fluorescent light streaming in and listened to the scurrying sounds of hospital care. And waited.

Eventually, a staff person entered and stood before us with a clipboard, followed by another, and another, and yet another. A nurse, a nutritionist, a social worker, and a mental health therapist. All smiled caringly, spoke clearly, and each gave Phyllis a survey to complete.

And then we waited again. Phyllis's eyes were filled with confusion, concern, and questions for which she didn't have words. I responded with wisecracks, but I seemed to be the only one who thought they were funny. Just as I was about to find someone to update us, the Renowned Researcher's nurse walked through the open door.

Finally.

She smiled like the others. "The preliminary tests show you're not quite ready. The transplant needs to be postponed, so we're going to discharge you." She then outlined the reasons, which I didn't hear. I was stunned. I looked at Phyllis whose body had slumped like a punctured balloon.

"Come back in two days," said the nurse before she left.

After completing more forms, we found ourselves standing on the sidewalk in front of the hospital wrapped in Central Florida's blazing sun at a loss for how to fill the interim. What would we do for two days?

Over the next forty-eight hours, we strolled through a shopping mall, which seemed ludicrous under the circumstances. I read *Crystal Enlightenment* to Phyllis—a book all about healing properties—and we discovered a park tucked between the highway and the hospital. We wandered paths that circled back upon themselves in a white-green mini-forest of wind-battered trees with twisted limbs. I expected a family of unicorns.

At last, we readied for Phyllis's return to the hospital.

"Do you need an anti-anxiety pill?" I asked.

"No, I'm fine."

I didn't believe her, and so added, "A half?"

"No, I'm okay."

Phyllis was assigned a room similar to the previous one. Like before, I arranged all the orange-tied tote bags—the ones with her clothes in plastic bags—and sat in a straight-backed chair next to her. We waited and waited. Eventually, an assistant greeted us with a pleasant smile and the news that Phyllis had been assigned another room.

We gathered the tote bags and followed him to another floor. An hour passed, and just when I thought the Renowned Researcher would certainly visit Phyllis, another assistant entered to move us to yet another room on another floor. We groaned, and with a laugh, Phyllis asked for the anti-anxiety pill.

Patience won out, because the last and final room for Phyllis's transplant was the size of an apartment. Three beds could easily fit side-by-side and there would still be room to walk around. Sunshine spilled through a good-sized window, creating diagonal patterns across the recliner nearby.

"Well, you lucked out," I exclaimed as I once again arranged the orange-tied bags and plopped the tropical flamingo tote on the visitor chair next to her bed.

Nurses and assistants bustled in and out. One demonstrated the sanitary washing procedures at the station outside the room and handed me the required gloves and caution-yellow protective covering that looked like a rain poncho. They settled Phyllis in her bed as it would soon be time for her first round of high-dose chemotherapy.

"I'm going to the cafeteria," I said, wondering to myself if I was really hungry or trying to get away from tubes or needles or shunts, or whatever they would do. "I'll be right back."

By chance, my cell phone rang while I was downstairs in the common area, something that might not have happened in Phyllis's insulated room. A Washington D.C. client requested I facilitate a workshop the following day.

"Sorry for the last minute," he said. "It's a bit of an emergency."

I replied that I was in Tampa, which he considered to be fine because the airport was as accessible as Atlanta's airport. "I'll get you a ticket," he said.

How would this work? What about business clothes? I was wearing shorts and tennis shoes. What about my car parked at Phyllis's house? "I'm with my friend who has cancer," I said. "She's having a stem cell transplant."

I repeated myself several times, emphasizing "cancer" and adding "terminal," because my client didn't seem to understand. Finally, I spoke firmly. "I can't. I'm sorry, I won't be able to be in D.C. tomorrow."

When I returned to Phyllis's room, she had me unload the tropical flamingo bag, which generated *oohs* and *aahs* and giggles between us. Photographs! Packs of them: our antics at Kiki's pool, our celebration at Kiki's second and successful marriage, the 1996 international games, St. George's Island, the Apalachicola house, her family, her pets. And cards and notes from former students, friends, and teachers.

"Get the tape," she directed. "It's at the bottom of the bag, and please collage them on the wall across from me."

When finished, I stepped back to admire my work. "Now, every time you look up, you'll see all the people who love you."

I turned to find her eyes half closed. The chemo had been coursing through her body since late morning, and now the bright sun had dimmed to dusk. I gathered my things, kissed her on the forehead, and returned to the apartment.

The next morning when I entered her room, Phyllis called me "her pig-tailed angel" as I sat on the edge of the bed. She appeared small and weak, a sick gray kitten in the middle of a huge hospital bed. In a raspy voice, she told me she was up all night, vomiting.

"Why didn't you call me?" I asked. But I felt relieved. I would have gagged and vomited myself.

"I knew you needed rest because you have a long drive ahead of you to-day," she whispered as her eyes closed. "They've given me the pain and sleeping medications."

As a result of the delayed start to her treatment, Phyllis had only been in the hospital two days, and my week was already over. Vince was on his way; the relay team was in full motion. I wondered about being spared the bulk of hospital time. Was it a gift from the Universe knowing how squeamish I could be?

"You were the perfect person for all the uncertainty," Phyllis said in halt-ing speech. "Vince, and especially Marc, would have gone stir-crazy. Can you imagine them going to a shopping mall?" She *sssssed* a sliver of a laugh.

I leaned in to hug her goodbye, but tubes poked out all around her, so I held onto part of her upper arm. There was nothing to her, no muscle, no strength. How would she make it through this ordeal? But as I backed out of the room, I offered reassurance. "I feel most encouraged," I said.

"Really?"

"Yes," I replied, and felt for the first time that I meant it.

Days later, I called. Phyllis's voice was less than a whisper. "I'm okay. My brother is here. He's watching the ballgame. That's all I can say."

The next time I called, Vince told me she couldn't talk. "She's having a difficult day."

Three days later, Marc answered my call. His voice was clipped. "She's okay, but she can't talk. You can call, but she literally cannot speak."

Two weeks later, Phyllis was released to the apartment. Joan, the sensible Dancing Girl, would care for her during this transition. They checked in at the outpatient clinic each day.

Email [from Joan listserv]

Date: Wed, 14 Nov 2001 18:21:45 EST

As hard as it is for her, Phyllis will have to depend on others. She can give herself a sponge bath, go to and from the bathroom on her own, get in and out of bed (slowly and painfully) by herself, and get a drink or a bite to eat from the refrigerator.

Her schedule revolves around the meds and for the next several days, the IV antibiotics, which must be administered by a home health care nurse early in the morning and again in the evening. She's hooked up to an IV for an hour and a half in the morning and for forty-five minutes in the evening. It really limits her daily activity.

She will need to follow up with the doctor about her pets and the animals' dander.

When Phyllis comes home, she will be in near quarantine conditions. No one can come in without washing their hands immediately, and no one can enter the house with a cold or other illness or have been around somebody who is sick.

When Phyllis leaves the house, she must wear a mask. We called it the Donald Duck mask because it has a bill that comes over the mouth and nose.

When we eventually spoke, Phyllis no longer had her usual lilt in her voice. "They told me the transplant went okay," she said, "but they won't really know for a couple of months. I'm a newborn baby, completely bald, and just sleeping, pooping, and learning to eat again. It's hard to walk. I am going to have to get a cane. But I feel like I'm progressing, not just surviving."

Email [from Joan listserv]

Date: Fri, 16 Nov 2001 15:10:40 EST

Phyllis is eating miniscule amounts of very limited food. Her tongue is still very sore (she says that she is still shedding pieces of it), so it is hard to get anything down that isn't very soft or liquid. Can't eat anything beyond lukewarm—nothing spicy, has no taste for chocolate or anything sweet.

They will be pumping the heavy-duty antibiotics into her through 11/21.

Her right knee, where the arthroscopic surgery was done, is very swollen and very painful. She needs help getting up and down from a chair. Her left foot is also still swollen and painful. But by yesterday morning she was walking from room to room without her cane.

I waited for Phyllis to return home before I called again. It had been almost four weeks since I handed her care off to Vince. Her voice sounded stronger when she told me, "I cried when I walked through my front door. I'm back in reality. Everything else was a horrible nightmare."

A nightmare? I wanted to know what happened during the weeks after my caregiver turn, so I nudged her for details.

"I don't want to talk about the transplant," she said, with long pauses between words and gasps for breath. "Remember the Vietnam vets? When they came home, they didn't want to talk. Then after some time passed, or something happened, or something sparked it, they did. That's how I feel. Maybe I'll be able to talk about it at another time. I just can't talk about it now."

CHAPTER 15

New Job, New Home

THREE MONTHS AFTER the stem cell transplant and five days before Valentine's Day 2002, Phyllis sent each of the Dancing Girls a handwritten card with drawings surrounding and interweaving the text like a page from a child's activity book.

> *You keep me floating like* . . . followed by the drawing of a feather.

> Self-portrait wearing a turban and dangling earrings with *I always wanted to be a gypsy.*

> In the center: *Dear, Dear Friends: I want to be the first to wish you all a Happy Valentines' Day. So much love has come my way. I am overfl owing and send it back to you.*

> Around the margins: *I feel like a million but one at a time, Mae West.*

> Ending with: *Again and again, Tha nk You All* and the drawing of a hand with two raised fin gers and *Peace.*

Phyllis and I had changed our phone call date from Wednesdays to Sundays because we both seemed to be too busy during the week. The conversations were short and didn't include stories about her recovery. For all the discussion and angst, and the post-care "musts" for transplants—*must* wash hands with antibacterial soap, *must* store food properly, *must* disinfect home, *must* keep pets at a distance, *must* limit number of guests, *must* use masks and gloves—Phyllis's life seemed to go on as usual. She mentioned her daily walks and a modified yoga class, but never spoke about her time at Moffitt or the experience she likened to the trauma of a Vietnam vet. Our lives returned to "before cancer," Phyllis in Tallahassee and me in Atlanta.

In early March, the Dancing Girls received a note with a drawing of Phyllis atop a dishwasher, thanking us for our gift to help her truly sanitize her dishes.

> Dearest friends, What a wonderful present! My dishes smile and my artist, dish-pan paws are starting to look like hands. I want to celebrate you, fabulous angels, in the spring when I'm stronger. I will cook Italian, and Dexter (the dishwasher's name) will take care of the dishes. Love (drawing of a feather) Phyllis...and we will dance.

The party invitation arrived in April, Phyllis's birth month, with a feather glued to its corner. Phyllis had drawn herself in her "Billie Holiday" dress wearing a beaded flapper cloche and kicking up her heels with her dance partners, her dog, and her cats.

> Let's celebrate my recovery and you! Please come to a party—make that two, one in Tallahassee and one in Apalachicola. Please wear your dancing shoes unless you want to go barefootin'.

I cleared my calendar, excited to gather with my friends again. The day of the party, I arrived at sundown, parked along the street, and knocked over things trying to quickly get out of my car because strains of "Last Dance" were vibrating out from the house and into the yard. Through the windows, I saw the Dancing Girls bouncing and gyrating to Donna Summer.

When I crossed the threshold: freezeframe. Everyone halted mid-move—someone even turned off the CD player—and a burst of greetings erupted. Hugs, squeals. It had been so long and so much had happened. I felt like a visiting dignitary.

Phyllis's hair had grown back to her ears, a boy's do, and she wore a wreath of glittered ribbons like a maiden in a Shakespearean play. Lights were strung across the deck where the "Laying on of Hands"—now a distant memory—had taken place.

I visited with Vince and Marc who made a brief appearance before leaving for a movie—or was it a sports event? I greeted Phyllis's mother, whom I found roosting in her usual seat at the kitchen table. Before long, the dancing resumed, drifting late into the night along with the promised Italian food—vegetarian, of course—and birthday cake and presents for Phyllis. My favorite was a stylized mermaid on metal, the length of a toddler.

The next day, Phyllis and I, the only participants in the second party, drove in her van to the Apalachicola house for the Tour of Homes.

"My art gallery is on the tour," Phyllis said, and probably in response to my wide-eyed look, added, "Anyone can have an art gallery." She thrust a piece of paper at me. "I called the newspaper. This is what the ad says."

I scanned her hastily scribbled note.

> There will be an art exhibit in town this Saturday, May 4 from 3-6 p.m. "On Apalach Time" art works are by Phyllis Bosco, including hand-made paper, painting, sculpture, and photography. The location is 112 Fourth Street. Behind the telephone building.

We hung Phyllis's artwork in the front room—the one I had imagined as a studio—and set up a parade of *Shamamas,* the palm-frond magical sculptures with horseshoe faces, to welcome the expected guests. The next day, morning sunshine gave the scene luster and pizazz.

Before the tour started, I went to the historic Trinity Episcopal Church on the corner of 6th and Avenue D. Two years prior, my meditation practice had led me back to the church of my childhood. Following Thich Nah Han's teachings, I had invited my ancestors into my practice, and sure enough, found myself drawn to the Church of England. "It's not unusual for Buddha to bring one to Jesus," a friend had said.

At Trinity, I sat on the left side of the church by the window, feeling grounded by its understated elegance. Maybe if Phyllis spent more time in Apalachicola, some of these parishioners could help her out with meals and such. Maybe if I got to know them . . .

An older woman with a long neck and white hair, reminding me of a heron, inched into the pew and asked, "Who are you?"

I responded with my name, but she asked again, "Who?" with a bit of annoyance in her tone.

I told her my name again and, thinking this was a great time to build Phyllis's caregiving network, I gave her a synopsis of my friendship with Phyllis and her cancer. The woman's face relaxed.

"Oh, nice to meet you, Phyllis. Nice to meet you," she replied.

I was about to say, "No, that's not my name. That's my friend, who has cancer and might need help," but then I simply smiled, nodded, and gave up on the church as a care network.

When I returned to the house, I discovered Phyllis wearing a tie-dyed shift and headband, sandals, and a shell necklace. Dangling feather earrings brushed against her cheeks. We were ready for our visitors.

A neighbor stopped by, toured the "gallery," and took our photograph on the white porch swing. Phyllis and I remained there and rocked, waiting. No one even walked by. Before long, I realized it was way past lunchtime—not because I glanced at a clock, but because I could hear my stomach growling over the squeak of the swing. In fact, Phyllis had set all the clocks in the house to different times to emphasize Apalachicola's timelessness.

"Let's go to the Gibson Inn," I said, "to celebrate the opening of your, um, art gallery," and we laughed.

We changed into sundresses, wide-brimmed hats, and dark sunglasses to dine on the hotel's veranda. Tall perspiring glasses of iced tea. White linen tablecloths. A wisp of a breeze, a waft of magnolia blossoms' lemony scent. The only things missing from our genteel Southern scene were white gloves and hankies. We walked home past the closed shops. In the window of one, I spotted an inflatable palm tree with luminous streamers for leaves. I had to have it.

"I love this," I told Phyllis. "It's so funky. If only I didn't have to leave today to get back in time for my job interview . . ."

A week later, I received a package: a folded rubbery pile with sparkling strands—my deflated bizarre palm tree—and photographs. I gasped at the image of us on the porch swing. Oh my gosh. We were once about the same height and weight. Now I was two of her. Our smiles were easy and genuine. Phyllis's fragile hand, with her long fingers, rested on my forearm.

I could tell by the interviewer's expression that I was hired even as she continued to ask questions about my experience. I would soon enter the telecom world, working for Cingular Wireless, my first for-profit stint: a nine to five—but typically more hours than that—lunch breaks, direct deposit paychecks, company-subsidized health insurance, sick days, and personal leave.

Six months ago, when I turned down my D.C. client, I hadn't realized that the refusal would lead to the end of my big contracts. And the smaller projects didn't produce enough income, especially when I had to pay for an individual healthcare plan. I needed a salaried position to survive. Goodbye to working from a home office and goodbye to flexible hours, which were critical for frequent visits to Tallahassee.

Also, goodbye to my artist-inspired loft and my downtown community. I purchased a condo in Midtown Atlanta for practical investment purposes.

A corner unit, one bedroom plus den, six stories up, facing Piedmont Park to the east and Downtown Atlanta to the south. An abundance of light streaming through the windows had me occasionally wearing sunglasses indoors, and it was quiet. No bustle of traffic and passersby, only the sound of barking dogs and the spirited call and response of birds. Peaceful, tranquil. Maybe a little too much. I had grown accustomed to the urban buzz.

I commuted to a multi-floored office building. I called it "cube world." My personal office space was three portable walls—slate-colored, padded cloth on frames—hooked together to my coworker's, which was hooked to another and another, and so on. Rows and rows like cornfields, but industrial gray and static. Strips of fluorescent tubes loomed above us, and way off in the distance, large windows provided a glimpse of the office park outside. I fluctuated between feeling too old for this environment and being energized by the youthful spirit of my coworkers. My biggest concern was accumulating leave time so I could be with Phyllis.

At home, my attention focused on setting up my new space: finding furniture with less girth for a smaller, cozier situation and figuring out plants for the balcony. A solution presented itself in the hallway by an elevator bank.

I turned the corner, and there stood a very tall, clean-shaven man with skin the color and texture of caramel. His arms held a crate of plants, still in their black plastic containers. I stared, disarmed by his striking appearance, handsome and larger-than-life.

"Hi," he said, and smiled with a grin that was both wholesome and mischievous. He leaned forward a bit, bending toward me, and introduced himself. He lived nearby, loved to garden, retired from pro-sports, and was *very* pleased to meet me. There was that smile again.

The five-foot-wide balcony that ran the length of my living room soon transformed into a lush paradise: shelves of pots, flower boxes, free-standing urns set on wheeled platforms; spiky, draping, and opulent foliage, riotous color, and ceramic birds tucked here and there. All thanks to my new friend who had somehow maneuvered his large frame around that small space like a dancer.

"I didn't know a gardener came with my condo," I winked, "I think I'm going to call you, 'The Gardener.'"

"You can call me whatever you want," he replied, a simple statement that somehow felt sexual.

E-mail [from Marc listserv]

Date: Thu, 08 Aug 2002 15:31:16

Phyllis developed a growth in her neck a week or so after she recovered from the flu. We saw the doctor at the Cancer Center. They did a biopsy and found it to be benign. She saw an ear, nose, and throat doctor here in Tallahassee and now will have surgery to remove the mass, August 19.

Marc's updates were grateful connections to Phyllis as I settled into a routine—with an alarm clock, for goodness' sake!—a commute back and forth to the perimeter around Atlanta, and phone calls with Phyllis on Sundays. I'd sit in the midst of my balcony garden, feet propped up on the rail, the phone tucked into my neck, while Phyllis talked about her week and asked about mine. Simple, often short, conversations between friends.

E-mail [from Marc listserv]

Date: Sat, 31 Aug 2002 16:37:53

The golf ball glob in Phyllis's neck was successfully removed. Unfortunately, the glob turned out to be a plasmacytoma, a malignant tumor. It turns out there are some myeloma cell clones that survived the stem cell transplant and are active in her neck and head. Otherwise, the myeloma is dormant throughout her body, as evidenced by her continued normal blood counts and general feeling of health and energy.

Phyllis will be back on thalidomide. As soon as two clinical trials are available at the Cancer Center, she will either be treated with "Imids" or PS 341, a cell-based targeted therapy.

Phyllis was finally able to participate in a clinical trial, something she wanted to do from the very beginning of her ordeal. The growths and "globs" were worrisome, though. I maintained a sick-in-my-gut feeling that things would get worse, a nagging ever-present sense dating back to Kiki's words two and a half years ago: ". . . she could live up to three years."

I wanted to visit more often, but now I was consumed with work. Summer had slipped into fall unnoticed because I was so immersed in the crisis-of-the-day characteristic of telecom competition with the latest devices, seamless number porting, upgraded billing systems, business customer service. My years of experience quickly moved me to the most visible projects, which meant driving home past sunset, waking up early the next day, again, and again. I kept my sanity with noontime walks to unload, complain, and laugh with a coworker. My bank account swelled, and my leave time multiplied.

Email [from Marc listserv]

Date: Wed, 16 Oct 2002 15:29:23

Since her neck surgery, more of these plasmacytoma lumps have appeared. She has five in all now on her shoulders, neck, head, and back. Nothing changed with the thalidomide treatment.

The doctors decided to try a new chemotherapy cocktail. She finished one round of this treatment and started the second round yesterday. The good news is that the lumps are shrinking, although the treatment is not fun. She's losing her hair again.

During our Sunday chats, Phyllis referred to her tumors as "bumps," and didn't say much more about them or her health. Her earlier words still rang true: "I don't want to always talk about being sick. It makes me feel sick."

We continued our calls, and even when the leaves on the old oak outside my balcony turned rusty orange, I sat there. It had become my special place for our conversations. I simply wrapped a blanket around me.

Eventually the leaves let go, leaving a lacework of bare branches. Another season had passed. Michael the Gardener pulled the annuals and readied the hearty plants for the below freezing nights that we had even in the South. In the evenings, I'd stare at the heavens, the galaxies of stars, and feel both connected and insignificant.

Most of my coworkers were off for the holidays, but I was saving my leave time to visit Phyllis in January. I became a mere dot in the rows of partitioned workspaces. The fluorescent lights hummed, and I'd hear an occasional voice without seeing a face.

Each evening, I turned off the twinkle lights on the twelve-inch fake Christmas tree that sat next to my computer monitor and thought wistfully of past Dancing Girls' holiday parties. I mourned in a way that only mothers understand for my sons' youth when they were always nearby. Now they were the ages of the Dancing Girls when we first gathered at Kiki's pool. My boys—I still called them that—were with their sweethearts this holiday and wouldn't be visiting.

The day before Christmas Eve, I stopped at Macy's before driving home and purchased a cranberry-red scarf infused with gold threads for Phyllis.

CHAPTER 16

The Last Art Show

PHYLLIS ENTERED EVERY art show in Tallahassee and was always accepted, even when her prospective piece was merely brush strokes beyond an idea. "I take a picture of what I have, call it a 'detail,' and send it in," she laughed. The upcoming show at LeMoyne Art Foundation was no exception.

I didn't, however, expect her late-night call with desperation in her voice. "I can't think," she stuttered. But before I could comment, she added, "I've always had trouble with this, and now it's even worse. Horrible. I can't do it."

"Okay, take a breath if you can." I wanted to say, "Calm down," but that didn't seem respectful, so *I* took a breath—a long one—and blew it out slowly, wondering what was going on. Was it the tumors?

"The art show, it's the art show. LeMoyne. The show at LeMoyne. Artist statement." Phyllis's sentences were choppy. She'd hesitate, I'd wait, and then she'd continue. "They want me to write an artist statement."

I found myself smiling. Of course. Phyllis avoided all formal writing like lesson plans when she taught, and she preferred handwritten notes scribbled on postcards. When she was required to take a basic computer class, the lab assistant significantly "helped" her so she could pass the course. "We need to go back to quill pens," Phyllis had proclaimed back then.

I continued to relish this memory while asking more questions. "Is it a statement about the piece you're submitting?"

"Yes, but it has to have a theme," she moaned, while I continued smiling to myself. "Whatever I write for my artist statement has to go with the theme of the show."

I wished we were doing this in person. She seemed so scattered and frantic. It could be the tumors.

I calmly replied, "I can help. We can do this together. Just tell me about the show and your entry. Just talk. Don't worry about the theme. I'll figure it out."

"The show is called *Wonder is the Beginning of Wisdom*." Both of us paused, letting that sink in before we laughed. Phyllis added, "I should be an expert. I've been wondering about a lot lately."

I reached for my notebook, scribbling—sometimes sentences, often just words—as Phyllis rambled. She'd stop mid-thought and repeat herself or gasp for air while I probed for more information or deeper meaning. I'd propose a sentence, she'd add to it, and so it went until we had a statement: *We're all here to help each other: joy, passion, turmoil, anguish, and humbling acceptance have the potential to intertwine our most intimate human relationships. Regardless of circumstances, the wonder of the human condition continues to prevail.*

Phyllis and I congratulated each other. Mission accomplished.

Email [from Marc listserv]

Date: Tue, 24 Dec 2002 02:12:39

Phyllis saw the cancer doctor last week. The thalidomide did not shrink or eliminate the little tumors—six in all. So the treatment was stopped. The "bumps" aren't bothering her that much, though one has grown slightly.

She had an MRI because she was having continued severe tailbone pain and a new sharp leg pain. The MRI revealed a 3-4-inch-wide tumor at the base of her spine.

Lumps, tumors, bumps! They're multiplying. They must be affecting her reasoning. I knew something was going on when we were trying to write that artist statement.

As planned, I drove to Tallahassee in January 2003 with the usual: music, books on CDs, my roller bag—this time with clothes for the art opening— and the tote bags with projects.

As I pulled into Phyllis's driveway, I braced myself. It had been nine months since I'd seen her, and now she had tumors throughout her body. But when she greeted me, dressed for the evening, I relaxed. She dazzled in loose velvet pants and a silvery top with a matching scarf wrapped around her head. Her perfectly outlined eyes had a bit of her old twinkle, and her lips were cherry red. She moved, and that's when I noticed her ravaged body: humped, unsteady, and dreadfully thin.

I hoped my expression didn't give away my shock and distress.

I drove us to LeMoyne and parked across the street. She held onto my arm as we slowly and carefully moved toward the gallery.

"Phyllis, you need a nifty cane like an African walking stick."

"I know," she replied as she focused all her energy on edging toward the two cement steps leading to the porch.

Blazing bright light poured from the open door and through the tall windows. A hundred patrons' voices blended into one conversation. I glanced at Phyllis, who appeared shrouded in uncertainty. Over the decades, she had been the headliner, the artist that admirers had gathered around. In her squeaky, whispery voice, she'd laugh with enough enthusiasm to toss her long tresses around her shoulders. Now, she had shrunk in both stature and confidence, appearing frightened and confused. I held onto her arms and practically lifted her up the steps. The crisp January air prickled our nostrils.

At the threshold, we blended into the slow-moving mass of bodies crammed into the hallway serving as a thoroughfare to galleries on the left and right. I pushed forward through the throng, leading Phyllis by the hand behind me, a bodyguard in pearls. Heads bobbed and friends called to each other. I continually looked back at Phyllis, nodding assurance as we merged into the crowd.

"Phyllis, Phyllis," a voice broke through the din. I recognized him as an-other local artist.

"Phyllis," he continued, I'd like to interview you."

Phyllis half-smiled.

"I want to know how you use your art to express your pain, to deal with your illness. Could we get together?"

Phyllis opened her mouth to speak, but no words came out. Instead, her eyes pleaded with me to handle this.

I stepped between them, grateful I had worn heels. My height met his and blocked his view of anyone else, especially Phyllis.

"Hi," I said. "We worked together one summer a while back."

I could tell by his blank stare he didn't remember me, so I launched into chitchat and held him captive as Phyllis escaped but not before whispering into my back, "I'm going to find my art and sit down in the other room."

A short while later, after I had wandered around the gallery, I discovered Phyllis propped in a leather chair looking diminutive but still glamorous in the way of aged movie stars.

"What was he talking about?" she snapped. "I don't do art because I'm sick. If I weren't sick, I'd do much more art." Her hands tightened around the chair's arm rests so her knuckles protruded.

"I know," I said, wanting to put the situation behind us. "I saw your piece."

"Yes. In the hall, not in a gallery," she scoffed. "Way, way back in the hall-way. You would only see it if you were exiting the building out the back door, and no one does that."

I too wondered about the placement and the artwork she selected: a per-son wearing a large-brimmed hat that obscured the face, dark with no trace of her lively Florida colors. It appeared even more somber by the dim hallway lighting. How poignantly sad, especially because I assumed, but didn't want to admit, that this would be Phyllis's last show.

For a minute, I wished I didn't have to work full time, that I could have been in Tallahassee, that I could have selected her piece for the show, that I could have personally delivered it and assured it was displayed in a prominent spot. But dwelling on these thoughts wouldn't change anything. I quickly returned to the present, a natural reaction from years of meditation. Right now, I just needed to be by her side.

The next day, a Saturday, we stopped at a blues fest and fair before driving to Apalachicola for the remainder of the weekend. Tents for performances and music lessons, artist booths, and fortune tellers were nestled under the oaks dripping Spanish moss like festival streamers.

"Let's get coffee at the concession stand," I said.

Mostly, I needed to hold onto something to keep my hands warm. When did Florida get so cold? Phyllis had given me a tweedy blue woolen poncho to wear. Her poncho was striped and layered over a thick red sweater. We added knitted hats. Phyllis wrapped a thick purple scarf around her head and donned her usual dark glasses. Arm in arm, I thought we looked like gypsies. I balanced two containers of steaming coffee as we slowly walked to the van, readying for the drive to Apalachicola. I noticed that Phyllis inched forward a bit like a caterpillar.

While I drove along the two-lane coastal road, I chattered about this and that. Phyllis simply nodded or *hmmmed* through partially closed lips. Everything had slowed down for her, especially her speech. Even more noticeable was her silence. The quiet that enveloped her was unsettling, but just the same, there was a dignity about it.

We stopped at Carrabelle Beach because of the restrooms, and except for the squawking gulls, we were alone under the stark, winter-blue sky. Phyllis indicated with gestures that she wanted to walk and took off, plodding along the shoreline. I watched her move into the distance as if it were the end of a movie, the heroine disappearing toward the horizon.

Fade to black.

After a while, I jogged up to her, grabbed her arm and turned her back toward the van. Before we left the beach, I photographed the shadows of our long, extended legs, disproportionate heads. Friends, side-by-side.

Once we arrived in Apalachicola, we walked through the streets to the waterfront, never encountering another person. A ghost town. Phyllis pressed on, slow-moving, struggling, silent.

That evening back at the house that was meant to be our retirement home, I found her upstairs at her sewing machine. How did she even make it up those stairs?

"What are you doing?"

"Making you a tablecloth out of Hilda's drapery material for the little table on your balcony."

Ah, those boxes at the top of the stairs. I remembered them from the first time I looked through this house, oh so long ago. Did I hear Phyllis add, "as a remembrance"?

Later, after we—mostly I—ate, we piled ourselves on the couch in the large room with the fireplace, no firewood. Feet-to-feet, legs atop each other's, and our heads on opposite arm rests, we cozied up in this chilly house wearing our ponchos and knitted hats. Phyllis's blankets outnumbered mine by three, and the space heater glowed crimson by her side.

Grinning and chuckling, I said, "Remember the art cart? We all experienced that at one time or another."

Phyllis nodded while her eyelids drooped a bit.

"At the end of my teaching career at Sabal Palm, I had a terrific art room, a suite actually," I continued. "But those art carts, oh my. My first teaching years were all via carts. I'd load the supplies from the storeroom and move on to the classrooms. At Bond Elementary, I even had to juggle that cart over the uneven pavement to the rooms without inside hallways." I laughed and Phyllis smiled.

"The desks were in rows, those desks with slanted tops. How in the world can you paint or do much of anything when the kids have slanted desktops? Paint could dribble right into their laps. I had a system, though."

Phyllis nodded more vigorously than before. I understood the gesture to mean *of course, you had a system.*

"Mrs. Williams—Lucille Williams, the principal at Bond—I loved her. She was a fireball. Short, stoic, soft-spoken. No one crossed her. And she did so much for the school and the community. She so appreciated my art carnivals. I'd pack the art cart with paint, brushes, fabric, and markers, and set it all up in Mrs. Clark's media center so students could go from station to station. You remember that, of course."

No response. I had lulled Phyllis to sleep. I wiggled out of our nest, dragging myself and my coverings to the side room with the daybed. I spread my winter jacket on top of my blankets and drifted off into a dreamless sleep.

CHAPTER 17

The Last Party

MY GUT CLENCHED, my neck tensed, and finally my shoulders drooped as I stared in despair at the email displayed on my monitor. More tumors, more pain, and so many other issues.

Email [from Marc listserv]

Date: Wed, 19 Feb 2003 04:25:22

After Phyllis came back from her appointment at the cancer center, two of her tumors—the one on her shoulder and the one on her neck—really swelled. Then a new bump grew on her neck. She started radiation treatment on the tumors.

She also has had a series of other problems. Terrible headaches, pain in her sinus cavities, and a sore throat. Her throat got so sore she could hardly talk and couldn't swallow.

Phyllis also developed nosebleeds and bruises because her platelets were low. She had to get a platelet transfusion. And she had to have a tooth pulled, and the surgeon failed to remove all the bone, which bothered her a lot until he fixed it the other day.

And then there were the words Phyllis spoke on our next call. She told me about her weak and worsening symptoms. Then, casually and with a bit of a laugh, as if to say, *isn't this outrageous on top of everything else*, she stated, "Oh, and I have a brain tumor."

"I'll be there this weekend," I said.

And so, unlike most people upon receiving a brain tumor diagnosis, Phyllis planned a party for Saturday afternoon at her Tallahassee house. Perfect timing for a celebration. Her son, Jimmy, would arrive that morning from Portland, Oregon for an indefinite stay, and I'd arrive after lunch.

I opened the front door to a packed room—husbands, children, girlfriends, friends of friends, neighbors—all lounging or leaning or standing in conversation bunches. "Hi, hi, hi . . ." Hugs, smiles, laughter, bustle. Carole pushed by me holding a salad large enough for a wedding.

"Wow, look at this," I said, standing between the dining area and the kitchen. A feast of vegetarian dishes vied for table space among containers of flowers and boxes of chocolate.

Phyllis's expression twinkled when she saw me, but she was swept away by a well-wisher before we could embrace. The scarlet red dress she wore hung formless over her cancer-thin body, and her complexion appeared sallow and gray. The cranberry-red scarf that I had given her for Christmas, which she strangely never acknowledged, was tied around her like a very long necktie.

Spotless, the dog, strategically mingled for optimum petting. The cats were nowhere to be seen.

"Oh, I see you're wearing feather earrings, too," Joan said to me.

"Yes, I'm keeping with Phyllis's bohemian look. I think she adopted the feathers from her new favorite book, *The Wind is My Mother* by Bear Heart," I replied. "Although she was into feathers long before she discovered that book." I now doubted myself and wondered why Joan was chuckling.

"Her father," Joan said. "The feathers are messages from her father."

"What?" All this time. Why hadn't I asked?

Joan continued. "Shortly after Maxi's funeral, a bird flew into Phyllis's kitchen. Phyllis believed it was a messenger telling her that her father was alright. She's worn feathers ever since."

Ah. I remembered the time we sat by the water's edge at St. George's Island, the evening before our road trip to Moffitt for the first time. Phyllis had told me about her dreams and feeling her father's presence. Now it all made sense.

After several hours, the party thinned until only the Dancing Girls remained. Kiki popped video cassettes of our parties into the player. The first three Anniversary Parties and the Student-Faculty Talent Show with our rendition of the "Pointless Sisters." What fun! We howled, sang, and interrupted each other.

Annie soon sauntered into the room with champagne. "A toast," she cried out as she opened the bottle and filled our glasses, some plastic, some crystal. We naturally gathered around Phyllis, although I'm not sure what we expected.

Phyllis's hand and voice shook. "Here's to . . . Pointless-ness."

Her statement was so sorrowful that it jolted us back to reality. Was she talking about her life, her illness? A cloud fell over our circle of girlfriends. No one spoke. With downcast eyes we sipped the champagne. After a while, someone picked up the conversation in a subdued voice. No more raucous laughter. Phyllis appeared oblivious. Maybe it was the brain tumor. Did she hear the word, "pointless," and fixate on it? We'd never know.

As day faded into evening, someone flipped on the overhead lights, which seemed to signal the end of the party. We hung around a bit, and just as it appeared some were about to leave, Phyllis dragged out the tote bags. The projects! Finally.

Years of photographs. We sorted them into piles. Family and friends. Any photo without a person—landscapes, houses, sunsets—went into the trash. A large bag packed with family photos and unfinished albums was set aside for her brother and her son.

The Dancing Girls left, and Phyllis and I were alone. Marc had long ago isolated himself in the den, and Jimmy had retreated to the art studio where he had set up an apartment for himself. Phyllis and I eased ourselves onto the soft-cushioned sofa, which now faced her fireplace. She had changed from the red dress into a faded denim shift. Her blue polka-dotted bandana was around her head. My favorite Raggedy Ann doll with the serious face and thinning hair hung from a hook on the mantel. We had planned to watch the news and Saturday Night Live, but instead we talked in hushed voices.

"The other morning, I couldn't get my head off the pillow," Phyllis said. "It was so heavy. I thought, am I dead? And all I could think of was the things I hadn't finished. Eventually, my eyes moved behind my eyelids. Then slowly my eyelids opened. I looked around and said, 'I guess I'm still here.'"

I had to smile. "Are you afraid?" I asked.

"The only thing I'm scared of is gross suffering. You know. If this lump in my neck grows out. Will it be grotesque? Or what if the tumors in my sinuses start growing out of my face?"

I winced, trying not to show it.

"I know I need to get up and do things. My anxiety closet needs to be cleaned out."

I smiled, picturing Phyllis throwing anything that caused her anxiety into that closet—the inch-thick manual for the required computer class, her wedding album . . . She'd simply open the door, and with her back turned, toss the item over her shoulder.

"I don't like the pain medication," Phyllis continued. "I just want relief from the pain, but I don't want to be a zombie. I don't want to be out of it all the time."

I had questions but felt uncomfortable asking. Finally, I jumped in, stumbling over my words, "What about your, um, clothes and stuff . . . ?"

"The Dancing Girls can have whatever they want, and then, well, give them to the women's shelter or something like that."

We sat in silence for a while. I stopped my mind from thinking about distributing Phyllis's unique possessions. I couldn't imagine tumors jutting out of Phyllis's face. Please God, don't let that happen.

Phyllis cleared her throat. "Sometimes, I wish it were four years ago. That was my life. That was real. This is not my life. This is just a nightmare."

The next morning, Phyllis walked me to my car. "Thank you for being my sister," she said.

"I love you," I replied. "I'll be back in a couple of weeks."

Her eyes brimmed with tears. "I love you, too."

Once in the driver's seat, I looked over at her as I had done after all my visits before driving up the hill. She stood, not moving, stuck. I waited for the peace sign, but this time I was the one to flash it. She waved it back and lumbered up the path to her front door. The woman who had peered out from the photographs we sorted last night, the one with the face-framing long hair and sparkling eyes, the one with the generous smile, no longer existed.

CHAPTER 18

Final Appointments

TWO WEEKS LATER, Carole called me in Atlanta after Phyllis's last appointment with her Tallahassee oncologist.

"Bizarre," Carole said, "just so bizarre and sad," her voice breaking up.

I reached for my ever-present notebook as dread twisted inside me.

"Phyllis lit into him. Really. She faced him from across his desk and told him doctors weren't treating cancer patients like they should be treated. Waiting rooms should be filled with music, and flowers, and exercise bikes."

I couldn't help but laugh.

"Wait, there's more. She handed him an envelope that I believe contained her Living Will, and when she reached across that barrier of a desk, a feather flew out and floated upward."

Now Carole was laughing, and I imagined Phyllis throwing handfuls of colorful feathers all over the office.

Carole got her bearings and continued. "The feather, the feather was now falling . . ." she started laughing again. "I thought it was going to land on his head, but then it rested on his desk right in front of him."

I figured this was the end of the story, but then Carole added, "Phyllis left to go to the restroom, and I went to copy some receipts for her. The doctor followed me down the hall to the copier. He told me the brain tumor is really growing. It's in her frontal lobe, so it will, and is, impairing her judgement."

I wrote "frontal lobe" in my notebook, as Carol continued in a soft, serious voice, "I think her cancer is all through her body now and the medications aren't working. That may be why the Moffitt Center isn't returning Marc's calls. I believe she's run out of options. We need to bring in hospice. I brought it up with Phyllis, but she's refusing. She said she doesn't want strangers in her home. Maybe you can convince her."

I sighed. "Okay."

While sitting at my computer, I researched, "brain, frontal lobe" and wrote in my notebook: *Front part of the brain involved with planning, organization, problem solving, personality.* I underlined "personality" several times.

Phyllis called me at work. This must have been urgent because she never called the office. I found an empty conference room and listened while she prattled on for the next hour. One topic after another in halting sentences, sometimes inaudible because of her hoarse whisper. Her struggles to think straight, the necessity of a million notes to just remember things, the danger of too much medication . . . and on and on. As her voice threatened to disappear, she eked out what sounded like her current refrain.

"I need to keep moving. I need to keep going. Dance, dance. I need to dance. I need to go outside. I need to keep moving." She gasped for breath, then continued. "I decided what my job is. My job is to keep moving in a positive way." She ended with a groan like a runner collapsing after a race.

I didn't know what to say and hoped just being available to listen was enough. I rambled about understanding the best I could, not being able to imagine what she's going through, that I loved her, and she could call anytime.

"Thank you. Goodbye," she said abruptly and hung up.

I returned to my cube wishing I were in Tallahassee. I really couldn't imagine what she was going through and needed to be there for her.

Email [from Marc listserv]

Date: Mon, 24 Mar 2003 16:02:03

Phyllis is not doing well. She had an anxiety attack on Saturday. She said that she is not taking any more drugs and not going back into the hospital.

The immediate crisis passed but her vision has become blurred. She has pain in the back of her head and is having trouble getting around because her legs and feet are numb.

We contacted hospice. We decided to keep her on dexamethasone, which will help reduce inflammation; to finish the antibiotics, and to continue a sleeping pill and the anti-depressant. She is off thalidomide and all other pills. She was obsessing about her pill, exercise, and eating schedule, which culminated in the breakdown on Saturday.

She is shaky and weak but continues to walk as much as possible. She wants to die at home.

Her last hope is a clinical trial drug PS341, or Velcade, that's waiting approval at the cancer center. They said sometime in April. She would have to go down there for three weeks at a time.

"This is absurd." I said aloud to myself. In one paragraph Marc wrote they contacted hospice and that Phyllis wanted to die at home, and then he mentions a clinical trial that would send her back to Tampa.

Totally absurd.

I immediately called Phyllis's house, but no answer. I called again and again, and left messages on the answering machine. Eventually Vince picked up, and in his usual calm voice said the Tallahassee oncologist told him that something would happen in a matter of weeks. This wasn't a shock, but still, it knifed me in the gut. Carol's call about Phyllis's last appointment had readied me. Yet, I still wondered about Phyllis's mania, that hour-long phone call just five days prior.

Then, there was another email from Marc.

Email [from Marc listserv]

Date: Wed, 26 Mar 2003 02:50:16

There is hope. The cancer center and the doctor's nurse explained their recommendation for the high dosage of dexamethasone as a treatment.

At first Phyllis rejected this treatment because she no longer wanted to take meds. But now that she understands more about it, she is willing to go forward with the high dose.

This gives us hope that her life can be extended. If she can hang in with this high dosage long enough, just maybe the clinical trial drug, Velcade, will be approved by the FDA in time for Phyllis to get on it. (For now, she is disqualified from the clinical trial since she has a brain tumor.)

This is also absurd. How could Phyllis ever qualify considering she has brain tumor? Did Marc think it would go away?

That Saturday afternoon, I pulled into her driveway. With long, determined strides I crossed the yard, knocked, and opened the door.

"Phyllis?" I called. Spotless sniffed me, wagged her tail, and didn't bark. "Phyllis?"

The house was hushed with filtered gray light, and rife with an unfamiliar metallic sour odor. I moved through the living and dining areas to the kitchen where Phyllis stood a few feet from the table. She must have gotten up when she heard me. She shuffled as I moved toward her, and there in the middle of a kitchen typically buzzing with activity but now eerily quiet, Phyllis slumped into my arms and cried. Her body shook, trembling with her sobs and then with laughter. I held her as if we were standing in the middle of a hurricane, sensing that if I even slightly loosened my grip, she'd blow away.

I glanced beyond her to the plate on the table with some sort of shredded cabbage in gray-green, milky liquid. Her lunch? How long had that been sitting there? Then, I purposefully took deliberate, even breaths. She soon calmed and her breathing mimicked mine.

Phyllis returned to her seat at the table. Everything felt off-kilter, tragic and confusing. I positioned a chair so that we were facing each other. I wanted her attention.

"Who's taking care of you?"

"Vince, Jimmy, and Marc, who's at the house in Apalachicola right now because he has a gig," she said in a very shaky voice.

I studied her appearance. I hadn't seen her in six weeks. Her face had swollen out of proportion to her neck, and her eyes were mere peepholes behind thick glasses, the kind worn by seniors celebrating one-hundredth birthdays. Then I noticed the most significant change. Phyllis was colorless. Her face and her clothes—layers of khaki and gray—mirrored the disgusting mush on the plate before her. Only a turquoise pre-wrapped turban, askew and revealing a few strands of brittle hair, interrupted her pale exterior. I sat there, shaken and speechless.

Then, as if struck by a revelation, Phyllis jolted toward me. "I'm crazy," she pronounced. "Crazy. Look at this place."

I turned around and truly surveyed the kitchen. Sticky notes and multi-colored file cards, all with scrawled writing in various marker colors, were haphazardly stuck—some with random pieces of masking tape—all over the wood cabinets, and especially around the phone.

"I'm crazy," she said again. Her trembling hands clutched a soft-bound purple notebook with large paper clips holding sections together.

She paused, sat back into her chair, and then jumped back at me with an eerie smile. "I've figured something out. I've been crazy all my life. All my life I've been crazy, so I became an artist. I became an artist to cover up that I really was crazy."

And then she laughed, a haunting, mirthless chuckle I hadn't heard before. Where was the Phyllis I knew and loved? An invading creature has sucked up her very being.

I heard a rustle and looked up to see Jimmy inching timidly into the kitchen from the art studio. He pulled up a stool, sitting awkwardly on its edge. We greeted each other with the pleasantries of people who hadn't seen each other for a while. I appreciated the relief of an ordinary conversation, and then Phyllis interrupted us.

"Crazy," she proclaimed again.

I had yet to connect Marc's email comment about high doses of dexamethasone with her behavior. I responded logically. "You're not crazy. You're unique. Look at all you've done." And I listed the art shows, her travels, the causes she'd championed, all the students she'd touched . . .

She jerked forward and shouted, "No, no. Stop. Too much."

I gasped and for a minute bristled, ready for a fight. I sucked in a long breath. This was getting to me. I looked over at Jimmy and marveled at his calm detachment.

I started again more simply. "You've shown people another viewpoint, another way to look at things."

"Is that my purpose in life?" Phyllis asked in a soft, but still haltering voice.

"Yes."

She clenched a pencil with a trembling hand and forced those words onto a page of her bulging purple notebook.

Then she lurched from her chair. "I'm taking a nap." She picked up an egg timer and turned the dial to ten minutes. Jimmy slunk back to the art studio.

A few minutes later, I peeked into her bedroom to find her sorting through a mammoth number of color-coded, marker-striped plastic baggies.

"My medicines," she said without looking up, to which I replied, "That was a nap?"

"I need to know what I have; I need a list."

"Do you want me to do that?"

"Yessssss." She stared at me, wide-eyed and annoyed as if to say *yes, you must do this now. Why are you even questioning me?*

Thankfully, we were interrupted by the opening of the front door. Vince strolled in, welcomed me, and without words—just the lift of his cheekbones and tilt of his head—told me they were doing the best they could.

"Phyllis is taking massive amounts of steroids," he said. "Then they are tapered off to almost nothing, and then upped again." He shrugged in a way that told me he wasn't for this approach.

Now that Vince had joined Jimmy, I could leave for the night. "I'll be back in the morning. I'll be at Wilcox's as usual." I hugged Phyllis, who was still preoccupied.

Oh, I needed a break.

When I returned the next day, Phyllis was calm, still trembling, but with a completely different persona. "She finally slept," Vince said. "I convinced her to take a sleeping pill."

With a grin, I asked Phyllis for "my list." She wanted everything in her art studio to be sorted, given away, or placed someplace else. It had to be a true apartment for Jimmy. And the anxiety closet still needed attention. "You can keep anything you want," she said.

I opened the door to the walk-in closet. Shelves lined the walls, but they were empty. Instead, everything was thrown into piles higher than my head.

I had my own list too. I clearly needed to take charge of details. Where was hospice? I thought Marc had talked to them. Vince and Jimmy had been vague. When I called, I found out someone had told them not to come yet. I arranged for them to arrive on Tuesday with an oxygen tank to have on hand, and they'd make regular visits after that.

Then, at Phyllis's insistence, I finagled an appointment with her oral surgeon for Monday, because she was certain he had botched the surgery she had last week; otherwise, how could there still be so much swelling?

I drove, then helped her walk up the path to the surgeon's office. It was 11:00 a.m. and she had already taken three pain pills. I knew this because, on her instruction, I dutifully marked the dose and time in her purple notebook.

The endodontist, a tall, grim-faced man with slicked-down hair, greeted Phyllis briskly but didn't acknowledge me. I took a seat off to the side.

"Tell me what's going on," he said to Phyllis, who replied that she still had pain and swelling.

"Well, okay let's have a look at your mouth." He was visibly pleased. "This looks good. Excellent. It has healed very nicely."

Phyllis gripped her shaking hands together. "B-b-but the swelling," she stammered.

"It's the steroids," he said definitively. "What are you taking?"

Phyllis relayed the steroid routine in a faltering voice, while the surgeon responded with rapid-fire questions about dosage and frequency.

"What is this steroid regime supposed to do?" he asked.

What a simple, straight-forward question. Why hadn't I asked that of Vince?

"It's s-s-supposed to slow the g-g-rrowth of the tumors." she stammered again.

"And then what?"

"I can qualify for a clinical trial."

"What kind of trial?"

"Well, they may have one soon. I would have to qualify."

"So, you are following this steroid regime so you can qualify for a trial that is not yet scheduled and for which you may not qualify?"

"Yes."

For the first time he looked at me. He didn't say a word, but his expression begged, *can you help me out? This is nuts.*

I raised my eyebrows and halfway shrugged my shoulders. *Yes, I thought that too, but what can I do?*

He cleared his throat. "The root canal surgery went very well. It's healing quite nicely. You don't have an infection," he summarized. "You can stop taking the antibiotics. The pain you're feeling is most likely from the tumors in your sinus cavities. Your face is swollen because of the steroids. Your other symptoms are typical for high doses of steroids."

His disdain for the regime was obvious in his pinched face.

Phyllis squirmed, grasped her tremor-ridden hands more tightly, and spoke with long pauses between her words. "It is a plan I am following."

"Well, um . . . well, good luck to you, then."

The endodontist's assistant brought in a wheelchair to take Phyllis to my car. I was surprised at how quickly she accepted the assistance. The last time I was with her, she wouldn't even use a cane.

In the afternoon, Marc returned from Apalachicola. He signaled to me that the two of us needed an appointment. We needed to meet, privately, away from Phyllis in the small room off the kitchen. He needed to know exactly what had happened over the weekend in his absence.

I sat on the bed. He sat across from me in a straight-back chair balancing a thick folder of papers on his lap, which he slapped from time to time. I stepped him through Saturday and Sunday with an even tone as resentment started to clench every muscle in my body. I moved on to our visit with the oral surgeon and ended up bombarding Marc with the same questions Phyllis was asked earlier.

"What is this steroid regime supposed to do?" "What clinical trial?" How will she qualify?"

Marc's voice was whiney, high pitched, and frantic as he touted the miracle properties of the steroid program. "Just two more weeks, that's all, and then there's a clinical trial."

"Do you know for sure there's a clinical trial?"

"No, well, but . . ." Without looking at me, he murmured that he didn't tell Phyllis she'd have to undergo a bone marrow aspiration to qualify.

I was now seething. "And the brain tumor?" I asked. "What about the brain tumor?"

His fingers drummed the folder on his lap.

Yes, I could have felt compassion. I could have understood his compulsion to keep his beloved alive, to find that miracle cure. But instead, the anguish of the past three days and maybe for all the years of Phyllis's illness exploded inside me. I slowly and deliberately got up from the bed, crossed the room, stood over him with my face inches from his.

"Phyllis is going to die," I said.

I walked out of the room and out of the house.

The next day, I came by as I always did to say goodbye before heading north on I-75. Phyllis was lying on her bed surrounded by her caregivers, all the guys. She shooed them out.

I sat at the foot of the bed, facing her.

"Would I have done this for you?" she said.

I smiled and felt too uncomfortable to respond. How would I know?

She paused. I studied her face as if I could actually see her thinking and figuring out the answer to her own question.

"You would have had a process. Everyone would have a role," she mused. Then she had her response. "I would do whatever you wanted," she said with conviction. "In my head"—she brought her trembling hand to her chest— "and in my heart. I would do anything for you."

Tears brimmed in her eyes and mine.

I held her, willing her frail body not to shudder, because I didn't think I could handle any more intense moments.

Soon, she pulled back. Her gaze was now soft, her head tilted to one side. I sensed love, serenity, and a cloak of peacefulness. She was ready.

"Words cannot express . . ." her words trailed off into breath.

I pulled myself together as is my nature, a woman in control. I had a long drive ahead, and for now, my emotions had to take a backseat. I stood up, feeling grounded by my faith in a loving God and the divine order of things.

"I'll be back soon, not this coming weekend, but the next," I said with strange certainty.

CHAPTER 19

Yet Another Party

FOUR DAYS LATER—a Sunday—I sat on the floor in a corner at Macy's, my back against the wall and my purchases splayed all around me. I pressed my cell phone against one ear and my finger against the other in an attempt to suppress the chatter of shoppers and hear Vince whose voice drifted in and out.

"I wish I had better news," he said.

My body stiffened.

"Phyllis hasn't opened her eyes in days. She hasn't gone to the bathroom. The hospice nurse had to put in a catheter. I'm trying to figure out a better way to give her the pain medicine."

Oh, God. I felt helpless.

"She hasn't talked since yesterday. She just moans. It's constant now."

I should be there. I ramble, trying to think, plan, and talk at the same time. "I'm not home. I'm at Macy's. I could leave right away, but it'll take me a good forty-five minutes to drive home. Then, I could toss some things together and get on the road. Let's see, I could be there in, um, seven or, um, maybe more like eight hours."

"No, stay where you are. You have work tomorrow, and nothing is imminent even though there's a big change in her condition."

I heaved a long sigh. Of course, it's 5:00 p.m. If I left now, I would have to drive most of the way in the dark. Why would I even have to go home first? I could leave from Macy's. But it would mean driving at night for hours on end, and I couldn't do it. What if Vince had said, "Come right now, we need you?" It was easy to let him convince me I should wait until the weekend.

I muddled through the next day, Monday, April 7th, 2003, until twilight curtained Piedmont Park, the greenspace a block from my condo. I walked alone in the hushed light. The only sound was the *pat, pat, pat* of my shoes against the pavement as I rounded the lake.

A fairytale scene appeared before me, a glorious gift to my senses. A velvet blue sky mixed with the glow from park lamps and city lights. A halo above a row of trees with lacey leaves. Gnarled, twisted roots emerged from the ground and disappeared into black shadows.

When I returned home, I heard the phone ringing from outside my locked door. Hurriedly, I opened the door and picked up the handset just in time.

"Hello," I said breathlessly.

"We've lost Phyllis."

I recognized Joan's voice right away. I plopped down onto the ottoman. Quiet soft tears tumbled down my cheeks. Joan waited patiently.

"I need a picture for my mind," I said. "Could you do that?"

"Of course." And Joan recounted step by step the scene she had witnessed. Phyllis was lying on her bed, on her side, with one arm outstretched, and her legs were bent and propped up on pillows. She was wearing a T-shirt and the turquoise turban.

Joan paused, maybe to ready me for the next part. "She looked awful, not at all like Phyllis. When the turban came off, all the outlines of those terrible tumors, blueprinted for radiation, zigzagged her bald head."

I didn't expect that. Who knew what was underneath Phyllis's headgear?

"But now, the best part," Joan said. "Her eyes were closed, and her lips were slightly parted in a smile."

Wow.

We didn't speak for a minute, and then I said I'd call the Deacon.

Later I wrote in my notebook: *Phyllis, I'm drinking chianti in my favorite glass. A toast to you! Now I understand the park. It was so peaceful and incredibly beautiful tonight. I wished you were there with me, and now I know you were.*

I'll take care of things. I'll call the girlfriends. I better get started. I don't know who goes to bed early. Hey, remember when you and I were the only ones up at 1:00 a.m.?

I love you, my dear. I'm so grateful you're no longer suffering. A friend said that when you went into your deep sleep, when you stopped talking, your burdens were lifted. You became more spirit, less flesh. I like that.

Five days later, Michael the Gardener and I drove to Tallahassee for the visitation at Cully's MeadowWood Funeral Home. We returned for the service the next day. A woman with an aura of compassionate authority—I don't recall her name—said to me, "You'll be seated with the family."

I shifted my weight from one foot to the other, and juggled my purse, which rested on my shoulder. Without waiting for my response, she opened one of the programs, and said, "When would you like to speak?"

"Oh. Oh," was all I could say. I hemmed and hawed, before emphasizing that I wasn't going to sit with the family, and "No, I, um, don't want to speak."

A part of me felt disappointed. One inner voice said to the other, "What do you mean you don't want to speak? You've been practicing for days."

The other voice said, "I don't want to walk up that aisle in these dress shoes. The heels are too high. I'm wearing them because Michael is so tall—"

"You're wimping out," the other voice interrupted.

"No, I'm not. I don't believe I'm ready. I don't know what tone to use—preachy, sentimental—I don't know. I just don't have the words."

My commanding voice, the one that had spoken up for my dear friend, had moved on when she did. Our journey together was in the past, and now we were in the present, at her funeral. It was okay for me to be quiet now and take my place with the crowd of Phyllis's fans. The chapel was so full that folding chairs had been set up along the walls.

Marc's rabbi spoke first.

"I didn't know Phyllis was Jewish," said a woman in the row in front of us.

I smiled, remembering Vince's call while funeral preparations were being made. "What were Phyllis's wishes?" he had asked.

"I don't know," I had replied. "I thought she would have told you."

"I thought she would have told you."

So Marc engaged his rabbi.

The Deacon followed the rabbi with Christian prayers and funny stories.

Vince and Marc spoke, as well as three or perhaps four people in attendance. The funeral felt stiff. I wished there had been a band. I hoped we would have sung songs, maybe gospel.

Afterward, the mourners drove to Tallahassee Memory Garden, parked in the parking lot, and quietly walked to the far section of the cemetery. The gardens reminded me of a watercolor painting: a pale, cloudless sky, translucent grass flecked with tiny blossoms. Stalwart live oaks with outstretched limbs framed the gravesites, and Spanish moss swayed like Buddhist peace flags. A fly buzzed and then a bee. Meadowlarks chirped messages to their friends. Michael held my hand. Nothing was harsh, and even the primeval smell of earth at the gravesite emitted freshness rather than dank musk.

Raised on a dirt mound, Phyllis's coffin looked almost friendly. Sunlight caught the wood grain as if it were a set of new wooden blocks.

Vince had selected it. "The others were too ornate and too expensive," he had said to me. "I couldn't imagine Phyllis wanting that, so we went for a simple pine box, typically for Jews, and had the Star of David removed."

I adjusted my brimmed black straw hat while I scanned the crowd. Violet sat straight and staunch in her chair facing her daughter's coffin. Other family members sat in chairs next to her. Most I didn't recognize.

Two men in work clothes sitting on a slight hill off to the right, almost outside the cemetery, caught my attention. Oh. Gravediggers.

We gathered around the site, and I shifted my weight from one leg to another, waiting.

I didn't see Rabbi Blume or the Deacon, and I wondered if there was a

master or mistress of ceremonies. Then, as if from another world, the gut-
tural sounds of Hebrew prayers emerged through the trees, followed by the
Deacon's soothing voice. I wished I had a recording of his final prayer to the
woman he loved so dearly.

Time passed. Most of us were quiet and inside ourselves. A few made
their way through clusters of mourners, speaking in whispers. It felt as though
we were holding time at bay, uncertain about the next appropriate behavior.

The men on the hill were standing now, leaning against their shovels.

"Pssst. Pssst. Hey! Over here."

The bushes to the left of the gravesite rustled and swished. Hiding behind
them, Kiki frantically waved at me. "Come here. Come here."

I moved closer and gawked. The art cart. Kiki had loaded a typical classroom art cart with paint, markers, brushes, glue, and a king-sized bag of colored feathers.

"I got permission from Vince," she said. "What do you think?"

I smiled and nodded. "Of course!"

Kiki joggled the cart over the uneven ground and stood before the
mourners. "I have an announcement to make. We all know Phyllis as an artist,
a teacher, and a promoter of the arts in all things. Art was her life. Her life was
art. Let's celebrate her life! I have no doubt that this is what she would want
us to do. Here are your supplies." She waved her hand over the glorious array
of options.

Turning to the coffin, she spoke louder. "Phyllis would have never tolerated this plain, undecorated . . ." She beckoned the crowd to come forward.
"Draw, write a message, leave a handprint."

At first, no one moved, which was my cue to select a marker and start my
personal note. I soon sensed a person to my right, and then someone with a
paint brush to my left. Before long, we were shoulder to shoulder, engrossed
in our tributes and oblivious to the others around us.

Kiki slid through the crowd handing out bubble-blowing soap with
wands, and cigars.

"This is just like one of Phyllis's parties," I heard Violet proudly say to another relative.

The men on the hill were now lying on their backs. One was blowing smoke rings to the heavens.

For a moment, my thoughts traveled back to 1983, to the conversation in the grocery store, and the drama teacher's lecture about the importance of funerals for healing. Now, I truly agreed.

My old pal, Loss, didn't accompany me to this tribute. Loss hadn't riddled my heart with holes this time; instead, my heart remained full. I had been a participant on a journey that had now come to its inevitable but glorious end, or so I thought.

The Saturday before Phyllis died, I returned from a yoga class to find Michael gardening on my balcony. He called to me. "Your friend," he said nodding at the pigeon nesting in the corner, "she left you a present."

There, on the cement right in the open, away from anything else, was a smooth, oval-shaped, gray feather.

"Oh yes," I replied with a flippant tone because I was so sure, "that's from my friend Phyllis." I picked it up and placed it in my childhood Bible, page 555, Psalm 23.

I didn't know then that the next day Vince would call while I was at Macy's, that he would tell me Phyllis's body was shutting down.

I didn't know then that he would say, "She stopped speaking."

The day I received the feather.

CHAPTER 20

Feathers at My Feet

A COUPLE OF days after the funeral, as I walked to my car for my morning commute, I discovered a gray and white plume—long and wispy—smack in the middle of my path, with no birds nearby.

Ah! Phyllis.

Over time, the ongoing communication persisted. There were "rules," which I instinctively understood. The feather had to be a surprise and destined for me. No one else could be around, not even a being of the avian variety, and the gift must be deposited directly in anticipation of my next footstep. Most feathers appeared in parking decks and pathways to and from home.

In the years after Phyllis died, I continued with my position at Cingular Wireless, which was eventually acquired by AT&T. I enjoyed the camaraderie of coworkers and thrived with the challenge of designing training for technical topics. Michael the Gardener and I embarked on our own adventure, but that's a story for another time.

This new era came with a certain loneliness. I had no friends nearby with a shared history who could make conversations easy breezy with no need for backstories or explanations. No marathon parties with the Dancing Girls. And no coastal roads in landlocked Atlanta for a quick jaunt to the beach. I viewed the many feathers I discovered as reassurance. *Continue in faith. This is the right path.*

Early on, I traveled to Tallahassee three or four times a year, especially in spring for LeMoyne's *Chain of Parks Art Festival*. Wandering along the boulevards adorned with artist booths nestled under ancient oaks was an excursion through my past lives. I could always count on bumping into someone I knew—the watercolorist from our 80s art group, the music instructor from my last teaching job, a professor from grad school, a parent from my son's traveling soccer team, and on and on. Often, I'd meet the Dancing Girls for happy hour. Vince would treat me to his famous brew of strong Italian coffee.

I thought I'd revisit our antics at Kiki's pool one summer, but I knew that was impossible as soon as I walked into the backyard of her new home. A smaller and more shaded space, a very different pool. Even the outdoor sculptures had been replaced with new and unfamiliar pieces. Most significantly, the other girlfriends weren't there. They were either busy or out of town. So on that afternoon, Kiki and I—just the two of us—sat in plastic-webbed lawn chairs, swigged beer from the bottle, and toasted the good ol' days.

Eventually, the number of trips I made on I-75 dwindled. I grounded myself in Midtown Atlanta, developing long-lasting relationships, enjoying creative projects at work, and taking evening classes at the local art school. My children married, grandchildren were born, my mother moved to a retirement community.

Still, when I least expected it, I'd find a message from Phyllis. *I'm with you. All is well.*

In June 2016, the most magnificent regal feather—deep purple with long fringe— appeared in the parking lot across from the Public Draft House on Peachtree Street, the venue for my retirement party. I felt a bit unsure and unsteady about leaving a career that had spanned thirty years. How could I let go of my rich friendships and satisfying work projects? But it was time, according to my financial planner.

Thirteen years after Phyllis's death and two decades after the 1:00 a.m. phone call when Phyllis and I agreed to purchase a retirement home together, I was forging ahead without her and without the house in Apalachicola near the beach.

I vacationed in Phyllis's beloved Italy and found a feathered message on a yellow-planked bridge in Venice. I wore Phyllis's draw-stringed pouch with the God crystal and sand from St George's Island while trekking the sacred path of the pilgrim across Spain to Finisterre, a place once considered the end of the earth.

More importantly, I carried the lessons I learned with Phyllis to the last weeks of another friend's life and to the last year of my mother's. Both women had limited communication, Pat with throat cancer and mom with vascular dementia. Now I had the ability to intuitively read the nods and glints in their eyes. I could serve as their interpreter like I did for Phyllis, sense their wishes, and take action on their behalf.

I knew to value our dwindling time, laughing with them, applying once again the mantra of so long ago: *laugh and enjoy the time you have left.*

When Pat became all bones, lying like a twisted branch in the middle of a hospital bed, my eyes saw beauty in her essence and unique Irish spunk.

As for Mom, I saw beyond her crumbling limbs and failing organs and glimpsed the child she had been. As I tucked her in for the night, a sweet smile lit up her face.

"Goodnight, Mom. Have wonderful dreams."

She'd always chuckle.

Just as I did with Phyllis, I held the hands of these two women as they faced their final days. And when it was time, I let them go.

Now I visit Tallahassee at least annually and stay with two longtime buddies, Kathy and Sherri, also friends of Phyllis, as it seems, is everyone in the Tallahassee community. I always request an excursion to the Gulf coast. Typically, we drive straight out Monroe Street to the Coastal Highway through Apalachicola, which still doesn't have a traffic light, and continue on US-98 to the tiny beach town of Cape Sans Blas adjacent to St. Joe's National Park.

Some days, we return to Apalachicola to wander through art galleries, chat with their owners, and check out the latest at Downtown Books and Purl. Phyllis's prediction turned out to be accurate. Apalachicola has indeed become an artists' paradise!

The Gibson Inn—the place where Phyllis and I shared afternoon iced tea after the opening of her "gallery"—remains welcoming with its wraparound veranda. The oyster and shrimp boats continue to line the waterfront where she and I last walked. The post office no longer closes for lunch.

Kathy, Sherri, and I always check on Phyllis's and Hilda's house on Fourth Street. We stroll by while visiting the galleries or peek at it from the van windows as we pass through the town. Different paint colors or changes to the front yard tell us new owners have taken over. Yes, we've considered knocking on the door but haven't yet plucked up the courage.

As we drive by the house on this visit, we find serious man-vehicles—motorcycles, a sports fishing boat, and an ATV—parked along the street and on the small patch of front yard.

"Phyllis has definitely moved on," I exclaim.

We laugh in agreement as we stroll to Café Con Leche a few blocks away.

I pause inside the doorway and grin. "She's here," I say louder than necessary. "Phyllis is here."

Of course, she would be at a café such as this, a wonderland of every hue imaginable. Mismatched primary-colored chairs at rectangular and round tables. A fire engine-red folding chair next to a mosaic-topped small table. Sideboards along the longest wall with baskets, racks, and an open vintage suitcase, all holding handmade cards for sale. Large-framed photographs of local scenes decorate the walls up to the ceiling, and unframed, splashy paintings with a graffiti vibe fill all the remaining wall space.

As my friends and I stand at the glass-cased counter, contemplating the attributes of either breakfast or lunch items, an older woman, wearing large sunglasses and a Jackie O style kerchief, hobbles in on unsteady legs. She orders her coffee strong plus a bowl of soup. Then she makes her way to a table, grasping the backs of chairs along the way for balance.

I watch her and wonder. She reminds me of Phyllis. The dark glasses and strong coffee are giveaways. I look around. Another patron, sitting in the section of the café that reminds me of a living room, is writing in a weathered journal. A stand of flyers is next to the door. Posters announce an evening of art for everyone. Phyllis would certainly have lunch here.

Later, I visit Apalachicola and Café Con Leche on my own.

I order a *café con leche* and sit in the far corner by the window, a perfect angle for studying the setting. This is what could have been. This is where I would sit if I had kept my half of the house, if I now lived in Apalachicola. I would stop by every morning, greet my neighbors, and write in my notebook. It feels right and true, except I don't live in Apalachicola; I live in Atlanta.

I have no regrets. The house on Fourth Street still needs renovation, and it's still too close to businesses, especially the mega gas station across the street. Sometimes, I have a pang of "what if" for the house with the trimmed lawn and picket fence. I wonder about purchasing it now. But such thoughts quickly dissipate. I've become more practical as I've grown older. I believe things have a way of working out.

When I finish my coffee, I'll get into my dependable white Honda and head north on I-75, leaving my musings, the beloved home of my soulmate, and maybe even Hilda, behind.

It's been almost twenty years since the party at Tallahassee Memory Gardens. Now, as I survey my condo, I laugh at all the feathers arranged as bouquets in jars and stuck in potted plants like appendages. There must be almost a hundred. Quite a collection.

Phyllis remains my companion in a new way, no longer geographically separated by highways and phone lines, omnipresent in her devotion. Whenever I open a book or a journal—I never know—a tucked-away feather might greet me.

Hello, I'm with you.

ACKNOWLEDGEMENTS

I'M SURE Phyllis's friends, family, and students each relive cherished memories when an unexpected song emerges from a playlist or an old letter is found bunched at the back of a drawer. And for some, recollections may be vaulted into the recesses of memory or even erased by time. Certainly our remembrances overlap, but the substance of this memoir is uniquely mine, reinforced by my obsessive notetaking in ever-handy journals. Much of the dialogue is exact. Pseudonyms are used for most names. For clarity, I've narrowed the girlfriend roles to four. In reality, there were more, varying in number over the years.

Phyllis's circle was wide: Debi Barrett-Hayes, Penny Yood, Karen Stanford, Dana Farmer, Mary Pierce, Stuart Riordan, Kathleen Wilcox, Beth Appleton, Joan Keen, Young Shin, Melissa Sykes, and Cheval Force Opp. Pat Curtis assisted Phyllis while she recovered in Tampa, wrote email updates, and told me the difficult news. Diana Anderson opened her home to us; Bonnie Bernau hosted the gathering at Alligator Point and took Phyllis to her last oncology appointment. I'm sure there were many others in her caring community too, people of whom I'm not aware.

I'm grateful for everyone who has contributed to this project: Janice Hoover, longtime friend and editor. You were onboard from the start in 2004. Deacon Jim Purks (1936–2018), you have a special place in my heart for years of encouragement and critical review. I thought of you often as I put the final touches on this memoir. (smiley face, glittery heart.) Hannah Palmer, author of *Flight Path* and instructor for the memoir classes, January to April 2020, I thank you for your encouragement, line edit, and for being my first reader.

Christy Bardis Petterson and Melissa Kemper Westbrook, you are my sounding boards, tuning forks, and my trumpets. I'm not sure what I would do without you. And now, Brynn Barineau, who more recently joined our Writer's Group. You all made this happen.

To Loosely Bound at Park Central in Midtown, Atlanta, the first book club to read the memoir: I'm grateful for your comments, your laughter and tears, and most of all, your friendship. Othene Munson, your challenge ignited the energy to complete the manuscript. Cheryl D'Amato, Claudia Hanson, Debbie Harris, Angela Masini, Margie McDowell, Marcia Rose-Ritchie, Sally Stieghan, Shawn Marie Story, and Emilie Sumera, thank you for always cheering me on.

Acknowledgements wouldn't be complete without thanking Indigo River Publishing. Georgette Green for seeing the future; Deb Froese for your editing expertise and kind counsel; and special thanks to editor Pat Smith who discovered the finest feather on land known for its raptors.

CPSIA information can be obtained
at www.ICGtesting.com
Printed in the USA
BVHW031808121022
649196BV00006B/14